Sharing His Great Love

The Life and Ministry of Nova Scotia Pastor Gary Manthorne

*Foreword by Dr. Harry Gardner
and the late Dr. Millard R. Cherry*

Heather Card

TESTIMONIALS

"Gary Manthorne will go down as one of Kings County's greatest ministers....because he treated the community at large as a church and has been treated by the community at large as their pastor, even when they have failed to 'darken the door' of a church."

— **Rev. Dr. Mark Parent, former N.S.,MLA** .

'Heather's book has made my eyes tear up at times, and I laughed out loud at other times, even when I knew what was coming because... I lived it."

— **Rev. Gary Manthorne**

Copyright © 2013 by Heather Ann Card and Lloyd Card
First Edition – October 2013

Original Cover Art by Kathleen Thomas (Miller)
Editing - Kenneth Miller (Actor) Co-founder and Principal of American Musical Theatre Academy of London, UK.

For information contact Heather at thecardteam@gmail.com

ISBN
978-1-4602-2680-3 (Paperback)
978-1-4602-2681-0 (eBook)

All rights reserved.

No part of this publication may be reproduced in any form, or by any means, electronic or mechanical, including photocopying, recording, or any information browsing, storage, or retrieval system, without permission in writing from the publisher.

Produced by:

FriesenPress
Suite 300 – 852 Fort Street
Victoria, BC, Canada V8W 1H8

www.friesenpress.com

Distributed to the trade by The Ingram Book Company

TABLE OF CONTENTS

iii	Testimonials
vii	Foreword – by Dr. Harry Gardner
xi	Foreword – by the late Dr. Millard R. Cherry
xiii	Acknowledgments
xv	Dedication
1	Introduction
11	Chapter One – Gary in Seal Harbour
27	Chapter Two – The Beginning of "The Call"
41	Chapter Three – Tales from Acadia University Days
49	Chapter Four – The Circuit Ridin' Preacher Begins his Ministry
57	Chapter Five – The Circuit Ridin' Preacher in the Gaspereau Valley
63	Chapter Six – The Circuit Ridin' Preacher in Pereaux
67	Chapter Seven – The Circuit Ridin' Preacher in Avonport – Lockhartville
81	Chapter Eight – The Circuit Ridin' Preacher at Bethany Memorial Church – Aldershot
89	Chapter Nine – The Circuit Ridin' Preacher in Clarence
95	Chapter Ten – The Circuit Ridin' Preacher in Seal Harbour
99	Chapter Eleven – 2009-2013 Four Years of Many Changes
107	Chapter Twelve – Roasting Gary – Some Funny Stories Lovingly Told
119	Chapter Thirteen – Gary's Darker Hours
129	Chapter Fourteen – My Interview with Gary
149	Chapter Fifteen – Gary, on Family Life and Roots

155 Chapter Sixteen – Conclusions
167 Author's Conclusion
173 Resources:
175 Obituary of Dr. Millard Cherry:

FOREWORD

- by Dr. Harry Gardner

The main character of this book has had a profound influence on my life. I was a young teenager when Gary Manthorne became the pastor of the Greenfield - Chelsea Pastorate in Queens County. My home church in Middlefield was part of that five point church field. He had my full attention on his first Sunday, when he began his prayer with "Good Morning Lord". It was not difficult to sense something fresh and real about Gary's ministry.

On my 16th birthday, October 25, 1969, Gary baptised me and a friend, Carol Dunn, who has also answered a call to the ministry. Gary showed a real interest in me and when I was 15, he took me to my first Baptist Youth Convention in Wolfville. I remember gazing up at the huge pillars of Acadia's University Hall and thinking, "Wow, this is a really big place."

Gary was somewhat involved with Charlie Taylor's prison ministry and he invited me to go with him to a Marathon at Springhill Penitentiary. In attendance were the inmates and those of us who came in from the outside. It was a 24 hour life-changing session for me and I was amazed at all of the stories I heard. Gary was always an encourager and when I was 16, he had me preach my first sermon at Middlefield Baptist Church. I believe it was about 5 minutes long.

I always knew I could count on Gary in any situation and I recall being stranded with a friend in Greenfield, where Gary lived, and knocking on his door late at night to ask him if he could drive me to Middlefield. Gary obliged as I knew he would. One of Gary's strengths is that he invests deeply in peoples' lives. When my dear friend Jim (a brother to Carol Dunn), was killed in a car accident, Gary felt he had let all of us down. He was on vacation in Vancouver and not available to be with us during that difficult time. Recently, when Jim and Carol's mother passed away, Gary took the time to be there and spoke at her funeral, remembering Jim and helping us to bring closure and God's healing in a wonderful way.

Other descriptive words that come to mind when I think of Gary are caring and non-judgemental. That is why I feel honoured to recommend this book to you. Heather Card has captured the essence of Gary's life and ministry in a way that gives the glory to God and shows how humbleness, empathy, integrity and servant-hood are characteristics that God can bless and multiply. She puts forth a side of Gary that allows us to see his empathy towards others, in large part because he has 'walked a mile in their shoes'.

If you are struggling with challenges right now, allow this story of triumph over adversity to encourage and uplift you. Gary Manthorne could have accepted his limitations, just getting by in life,

Sharing His Great Love

but he chose to develop a servant's heart, looking for ways to bless and care for others. Day by day he allowed God to work his grace and power in his life. Gary seeks to model Jesus, the greatest servant of all time.

In recent, years a highlight of the annual Convocation Ceremony at Acadia University was to see Gary assisting Dr. Millard Cherry to his seat. 'Cherry' has been a Mentor and Confidant to Gary and to so many other people. Sadly, for the first time this year, we were not privileged to see that familiar gesture as 'Cherry' passed away on October 5, 2012. I am honoured to share the foreword for this book with him. Like me, I am sure he would want this book to encourage you and speak in a way that would enable you to begin or strengthen your personal relationship with our Lord.

(Dr. Gardner's Bio is at the end of the book.)

FOREWORD

- by the late Dr. Millard R. Cherry

Author's notes:
On January 19, 2012, at 3:00 PM, I met with Dr. Cherry at his home in Wolfville, N.S. On that day his caregiver Darlene Gillam, from Newfoundland, was also there. I arrived with the introduction, several chapters of my book, and an invitation for Dr. Cherry to participate by writing the foreword of the book about the life and ministry of Rev. Gary Manthorne. He asked me to read the material to him after which he informed me that he no longer did any writing, but that he would be happy to do the foreword if he could dictate it to me. Although he seemed in some physical discomfort and a bit agitated, he said that we would start then and see how far we got. I later learned that his discomfort was due to a mix-up in medications. We didn't get very far and because of my schedule and Dr. Cherry's ill health, we didn't get a second appointment. However the following is what he dictated. I have also included his obituary at the end of the book, as I know it is important to Gary that Dr. Cherry is included here because of his great influence on Gary and his very practical help to him.

Dr. Cherry's Words as dictated to me:

"Although I agree that Gary Manthorne's ministry is unique and could be seen as untraditional in many ways, I want to point out that he had a good traditional ministry as well. Although I don't know the author very well, I believe she is sincere and that her purpose is honourable. I agree with her that she certainly has a story of triumph over adversity that a lot of people will credit to the glory of God.

I have a great deal of love for Gary Manthorne and to this day I appreciate his attentiveness to me, his regular visits and his friendship. Gary embodies some great principles and he has had a good ministry thus far. I am so glad that you chose to honour Gary in this way, Heather. Gary Manthorne will be remembered a long time by the many people that he has touched and I am delighted to be a part of a book that could help make that happen."

(Dr. Cherry's obituary is at the end of the book.)

ACKNOWLEDGMENTS

I would like to acknowledge and thank the contributors to this book. I could not have written it alone. I believe this book will have greater impact on peoples' lives because of the willingness of others to share how they feel about Gary's ministry and friendship. The contributors did not collaborate so there are some repetitions from different points of view.

I owe special thanks to Gary for the permission to embark on this project and his willingness to 'dig deep' into his inner being and re-live the many emotional scenarios that were necessary to give me the information that I needed. I want to thank him for his honesty and for trusting all of us with the sensitive issues of heart and mind that are sometimes difficult to share.

The contributors are listed in alphabetical order.

Ellen Beaumont
Rev. Harold Beaumont
Rev. John Beers
Annie Laurie Bird
The late Dr. Millard Cherry
Rev. Pauline Coffin
Lolita Crosby
Dr. Harry Gardner

Joe and Natalie Johnson
Bethany Keddy
Laurie Levy
Keith and Bessie Luddington
Charles and Gloria Manthorne
Rev. Gary Manthorne
Linda Manthorne
Rev. Dr. Mark Parent
Alex Smith
Dr. Alison and Gene Trites
Donna Turner

I would also like to thank my daughter Kathleen Thomas, for doing a great job of the original art work on the front cover of the book.

My son, Kenneth Miller, spent many hours editing this manuscript. I want to thank him for taking so much time from his already busy schedule.

Most of all I want to thank my Lord and Savior, Jesus Christ. While writing this book I have had many moments of looking up to him in prayer for inspiration, confidence and assurance that I was in his will.

DEDICATION

I dedicate this book with love, to my husband Lloyd William Card. This Book was his idea. When I came home from church one Sunday with yet another 'Gary' story, he said, "Heather, you should write a book. There are so many stories that need to be written down". Yes, so many stories that you would think it would be easy. However, writing a book takes focus. I owe much gratitude to Lloyd for keeping me on track and for looking after many every-day household tasks (and other duties) for me, so that I would have more time to write.

INTRODUCTION

Gary Manthorne is a successful pastor, although you might not think so judging by the size of some of his churches. However upon a second look, you can see that his ministry has probably reached more people than most of the pastors of today because he clearly has 'a church without walls'.

Gary's strength is his community pastoring. There is no doubt in my mind that Gary believes that God hates the sin but loves the sinner, and he also believes deep down (as the Bible tells us) that to God all sins are equal. This is something that I believe all Christians should know but it seems to me that there are people who believe that a sin of telling a little white lie, exaggerating the truth or gossiping, is way less significant than being a murderer, thief or an adulterer.

Wouldn't it be wonderful if we could see people for the way they 'could' be, and not for who they are right now? Wouldn't it be great if instead of taking away their hope, we could see them as God sees them and love them as he loves them? The Bible tells us that only God can deal with the sin. We cannot. As Christians, we are taught that no matter what we do, we cannot justify alienating someone because of their sin. We need God's grace to keep sin away from our own door.

Gary exemplifies this thinking in his ministry. I have never heard him preach on the subject but I see it in his every day treatment of the people around him. Why does he have such a great grasp on this? Why does it seem to flow effortlessly from him? Could it be education? Lots of pastors have the same education. It can't be just from reading the scriptures. Plenty of us have read those same scriptures. It can't be environment. Others have had similar. It can't be his struggles. Many of us have challenges to overcome. So what is it then? I think it is because Gary not only knows the scriptures, but asks God daily to apply them to his heart. The reason he is able to show God's love so humbly is because he knows that it is not him but the Holy Spirit working through him.

Whenever I ask someone, "Do you know Gary Manthorne?", before they go on to tell me their connection to Gary, they always smile. That would be a legacy that Gary would be proud of given his now almost effortless propensity toward humour.

When I first met Gary and observed his style, I had flashback pictures of the stories of Jesus in the Bible stories I had heard in my youth. To imagine Gary's laid-back manner and long, shaggy beard in those stories makes me smile.

"Hey fellers, if you're not catchin' any fish, why not try throwing that net on the other side? It can't hurt." Or (holding up his coffee cup) saying, "Zacchaeus, I need to have a bite to eat with this. Come on down from that tree and let's head on over to your house."

I first heard and accepted the gospel in New Brunswick in an area that was known as the 'Bible Belt'. All of the teaching I had was very literal and very evangelical. Prior to that, having travelled from Sheet Harbour with the United Church Youth Group, I had been exposed to a couple of Billy Graham's services in Halifax. Because I had been very involved in the ministry of music and youth work in the Baptist churches in New Brunswick, I had received a lot of good Bible training from the pastors there. I worked in the ministry with Rev. Harold Braun (even before the Rothesay Baptist Church was built) and with the late Rev. Eric Davidson in Central Baptist Church in Saint John.

When circumstances brought me back to Nova Scotia in 1982, I soon experienced that most Baptists here were not quite as openly conservative as I had learned to be. I carried my Bible everywhere and if I were in the car, my Bible was on the dashboard. I randomly quoted the scripture at every possible opportunity. I thought all Baptists did that because that is what happened in the church I came from. This will help you to understand my first reaction to Gary Manthorne.

In 1996, I met Gary and I just could not figure him out. First of all, if there were a country music song within earshot, he would be beaming and tapping his foot. In a group of people he would be the one with the humorous remarks making everyone laugh. A lot of his humour was pointed at him, not in a self-effacing manner but rather as if joking with an old friend. But there was some serious kibitzing with his friends as well.

In his church services, I never heard an 'altar call' (an invitation to come forward and give your life over to Christ). I always thought, "What is the point of this ministry?" I once even walked out of a Hymn Sing he was conducting when the special guest, obviously recruited from the Legion on Saturday night, began to sing a non-gospel country song that I thought Gary was enjoying way too much. I expressed to Gary that I was very disappointed that I attended a Hymn Sing at the church and there was no distinction between that and a Saturday night variety show. I thought a pastor would have stopped the performance and gotten it back on track. An even less liberal pastor would have thrown the guy out, like the way that Jesus cleared the temple, so to speak.

Gary expressed concern that I felt offended but made no apologies. When I look back, I can believe that Gary in his particular brand of ministry had seen an opportunity to bring a person into the church, however briefly, and show him acceptance and love without judgement. At that point he may have felt he should not need to minister to people like me who already knew and accepted God's love. Was I being like the Pharisees?

Gary seems to be able to see the wants, needs, interests and abilities in other people, never overlooking the 'you' factor in others. From a child who could not hear properly and therefore could not speak correctly, he has become proficient in his speech and puts thought and enthusiasm into the message he wants to deliver. As we know, it is difficult enough to endure the challenges life sometimes throws at us, but here is a glimpse of an unknowing child, teased by his peers, made fun of by their parents, living in a small community where laughing at him was community entertainment.

I have always heard, "Be careful of the words you speak. Once they leave your mouth you cannot take them back." In Proverbs 18:21, the Bible says, "Death and life are in the power of the tongue." In speaking with Gary of his youth, these truths became so real to me as I listened to the emotion in his voice and witnessed the tearing up in his eyes as he spoke of some of the things that were said to him by people who should have known better. I sense that Gary has made peace with those things, realising that nobody meant to destroy his confidence or to hurt him in any way. All they meant to do was get a laugh. If only they had been able to see that they were 'ripping a child apart' inside.

Perhaps Gary developed his own sense of humour to help boost his self-esteem. To be able to make people laugh is to be accepted in most circles where Gary finds himself - that would be just hanging out with people wherever they are, extending God's love outside of the church situation.

This story is not meant to be a biography but rather one that highlights the events of Gary's life, to show that when we give who we are and what we have back to God, he can use us for the purpose that he intended for us. Even if the vessel is broken, God can heal, pick us up and plant us on a road that ultimately gives him the glory. Between the lines on these pages there are many lessons that I hope the reader will find for encouragement, hope, and a deeper faith in a God who wants our lives to count for something.

About the title: "Sharing His Great Love"
Matthew 7:1-2
"Do not judge so that you will not be judged. For by the standard you judge you will be judged, and the measure you use will be the measure you receive......."

Gary Manthorne looks out for people on the outside of his church ministry as well as those who regularly attend church. Maybe you can relate to one of the following scenarios:

You were a 'believer' once and your life took a bad turn. Your past came back to haunt you and you slipped into solitude, drinking, smoking, and avoiding church. Now, you find out that cancer is ravaging your body and you may not have long to live. You need to reach out to someone you think can help you find that connection you once had to God.

You have a close family member who has never gone to church, who wants to get married. You want them to be married by a pastor because you think that at least a Christian marriage ceremony might bring them closer to God.

You are divorced and want to get married. Once you were really involved in church but you experienced a lot of hurt. You have been living for several years with your new partner who is also divorced.

You are a 'believer' and you have a close family member who is not a professing 'believer' who has just died. He was an alcoholic and his life was a mess. You feel the need to have some kind of funeral for family and friends just out of respect.

Maybe you have made mistakes in the past and you feel that others no longer respect you and you have a very low opinion of yourself. Perhaps you are angry with God, because your life seems out of control, through no fault of your own. You have some deep questions that you would like answers for.

In every instance you could call Gary. I have attended many funerals and weddings where Gary has presided without judgment. At a funeral, Gary always has a way of speaking about the deceased which signifies respect for the decency in them. He seems to have an understanding of their struggles, and therefore he is able to comfort their family and friends. He always assures those present of God's great love for them. I have witnessed some of the good that has followed.

In many cases I have seen people who have been touched by Gary's caring spirit, turn back to God. To see the love and respect that Gary has for people is to witness the love of God. Perhaps some of them have never experienced love before. I have observed that to share your sorrow with Gary is to diminish it by half and to share your happiness with Gary is to double it.

Gary has been the minister of choice in the economical backyard wedding fad. My own wedding to Lloyd Card took place in our back garden with only 7 in attendance, including Gary. Several years later my daughter Kathleen was married to Ronald Thomas in the same garden, in the presence of family and friends.

The Wedding of Kathleen and Ronald Thomas.

Gary Manthorne, started out with a challenge that would make a lot of people want to settle for just getting by, but now has a ministry that for over forty years has been, for the most part, within a forty mile radius of his home in Wolfville, Nova Scotia. His faith has overcome any fears or doubts he may have had about being a pastor and with God's guidance he has become a most beloved and respected member of his community.

About the Author's Notes

I hope you will see what I call the 'web of destiny' that is woven between these stories. I believe there is a connection, a moving of God's hand, not only in Gary's story but in the relationship of the author, subject and reader. This is not a case where a writer just picked a subject and wrote. Some of the people depicted in this book have never met each other personally. However, I would say that their lives and their spirits had crossed paths many times. I believe that this can happen only by the hand of a God who sees the whole picture, knows every outcome and the purpose for every interaction. If this is true, and not merely a hypothesis, then every contact with another human being is an important one. That leaves us with an awesome responsibility.

I wonder if it is possible that everywhere we have been, a part of our spirit remains and has an effect on those who come after? What if, through the choices we make, we leave ripples that reach one person and affect another person we have not yet met or may never meet? That very possibility makes me desire to leave something encouraging behind. Is there something that you want to leave behind as a legacy?

I do not believe in coincidence but I do believe in destiny. Therefore, I ask the reader's patience as I connect these stories throughout the book, to show 'the tie that binds'. I hope that you will be entertained by these reflections and that you will find a thread that will also connect you with the story in a meaningful way.

Epigraph:

"In the Church of the future, members will be just meeting people at restaurants or at the soccer pitch. Rather than asking people to come to us, we'll be going and just being a part of the world we live in."

Rev. Wayne Dryer, as he commented on the pending closure of the Germain St. Baptist Church, Saint John, NB.

CHAPTER ONE

Gary in Seal Harbour

Jeremiah 1:5 "Before I formed you in your mother's womb, I chose you. Before you were born, I set you apart......."

In the year 1945, at St. Martha's Hospital in Antigonish, Gary Manthorne was born on September 28, to Douglas Manthorne and Carrie (Hadley) Manthorne. The Manthornes lived in the obscure, little fishing village of Seal Harbour, on the Eastern Shore of Nova Scotia. The family home was on a wooded lot called Grandmother's Hill, although nobody remembers how it got that name.

The Life and Ministry of Pastor Gary Manthorne

The Manthorne Homestead -Grandmother's Hill

View from the Air

Many memories dear to the heart of the people of Seal Harbour are chronicled in the book "Where Seagulls Soared", which was compiled and edited by Bethany Keddy. Bethany, who jokingly describes herself as a somewhat, something cousin of Gary's on her grandmother's side, shares Gary's sense of humour and (like Gary) is quite a punster as well. Bethany's grandparents Beryl and Barney Langley were very fond of Gary and always enjoyed his visits. Barney was one of the men who rescued Gary and his friend from Goose Island on their ill-fated trip that you will read about later. Bethany said that her family felt very blessed to have Gary preside at both of her grandparents' funerals.

Gary contributed an article for "Where the Seagulls Soared", as did many of the residents of Seal Harbour. Here is an excerpt from Gary's submission entitled "The Way We Were." It illustrates very well, the particular brand of humour for which Gary is so well known.

"...........Kids had to help with everything in my day. Sprout the potatoes - they'd put me down in the cellar in March, the way I recall it now, and I wasn't allowed up again until I'd done the whole eight barrels. Chores were part of the routine. I was eight years old before I knew my name wasn't 'Get Wood'.

Cats were often favourite pets. They sure were at our house. I happened to be the first kid in Seal Harbour to go to the new High School in Guysborough in 1960. It sounded like a long trip to me, so I'd get tired just thinking about it every night. I'd curl up on the couch in the evening with the cat, falling asleep with my homework. Mom, ever the teacher, would come along and volunteer to read my assignments to me. The cat would listen with rapt attention while I slept. As a result, that cat became the most educated cat ever to come out of Seal Harbour. Come to think of it, the cat never came out of Seal Harbour. Mom and Dad kept the cat home for years and sent me off to the Valley at 17 to accumulate a mortgage. I guess the cat finished High School and certainly was able to live on successfully into old age, debt free on Grandmother's Hill.............."

Bethany Keddy gave me the information on the annual Seal Harbour reunions and Gary's part in them. She said that originally her mother, Kay, and one of Bethany's aunts, were looking at a school picture from 1949 - 1950 and decided to get in touch with all 23 people in the picture (which included Gary's brother Charles). The teacher, Pearl Fanning, had already passed away.

The first reunion was in 1984. After that, they were inspired to declare the first weekend in August as 'Come Home Weekend'. The reunions included picnics, hikes, fires on the beach, trips to Goose Island and a Saturday night show, with Gary as Master of Ceremony. For many years now, the festivities have started with a potluck meal at the Manthorne homestead on Grandmother's Hill, hosted by Gary's brother Charles and his wife Gloria. They culminate with the Sunday service (led by Gary) and another pot-luck meal in the basement of the church. A few participants even return at suppertime to finish up the left-overs and to say a final goodbye until next year. As the years go by and the population ages and dwindles, there are fewer activities but the Sunday service and the pot-luck go on. August of 2013 will be the thirtieth. The community really appreciates Gary's strong presence at the activities which of course he appropriately colours with his humour. His own memories of the reunion are as follows:

"One constant event has been the Saturday night program where anyone and everyone contributes music or stories and anecdotes of their Seal Harbour memories. I have enjoyed being the MC and calling on folks to come up front and do something. Harold Langley's family (from Cape Breton and beyond) often got there in one combination or another and delighted us with their skits, songs, and readings from Harold's diaries. Bob Giffin, a Goldboro native and husband of Laureen Latham who was in the picture (of 1949 – 1950) that inspired the reunion, kept us 'in stitches' with his impromptu comedy acts.

We could always count on three generations of another Langley family to contribute in a major way - that would be Beryl, and her daughters Judy Jolotta, Kay Keddy and Kay's daughter Bethany. Even well into her nineties, Beryl continued to keep us laughing about the challenges of aging, or reflecting on how times had changed in her lifetime of living 'literally' on the edge of the Atlantic. Each year, two or three people do not return, and in recent years, Beryl and Judy answered the 'Roll Call up Yonder', as have so many other dear souls - leaving us with wistful hearts and precious memories. Along the way, Bethany did us a great service when she produced the wonderful book reflecting

Seal Harbour life and memories, entitled 'Where Seagulls Soared'.

The second constant event every year at the reunion is the Sunday morning church service. It is always an honour for me to lead the service. We sing the old time hymns of our ancestors and reflect on how the stories in the Bible seemed so much like our own stories of life and death.

Other aspects of the reunion have varied. In the earlier reunion years, we made some voyages to the fabulous and famous Goose Island, where for generations kids were always told, 'It's not fit to land there today.' One year, we planted the Seal Harbour flag on Front Beach and claimed the island as a Seal Harbour territory. The flag was a gift of Ann Manthorne's creative generosity. Another summer, Bedford Pinkham ferried us there, anchoring his boat nearby. Eventually, we realised his boat was slowly drifting away, so of course he immediately rowed out and secured the anchor. You will find it fitting that one of the songs at the evening program "Drifting Too far From the Shore", was dedicated to the Goose Island voyage.

There were several reunions when we were treated to impressive fireworks down at the cove at the site of the old fish plant, thanks to Dennis Randall, otherwise of Chicago and /or Kendall Worth, otherwise of Halifax. In more recent years, until his health became an issue, Parker Langley started up Saturday morning breakfasts that stirred up some serious cash for the church. That tradition continued for some years with the old time volunteers that Parker had recruited.

So many times over the years, people have commented to me at Nova Scotia funerals, that a funeral is the only time their family ever gets together. Thankfully, when Kay (Langley) Keddy, and Herb Manthorne declared more than thirty years ago that we should all get together while we are still living, they gave us all a wonderful gift. We now have the opportunity to keep seeing each other - celebrating our heritage and traditions as we reminisce about the people and experiences of growing up where and when we did.

As a kid, I used to feel sorry to think of other kids growing up without a cove, an ocean, a forest, an island, a boat and a church family. To this day, I truly cannot recall a moment in my life where I envied someone for growing up somewhere else. Thank you, Seal Harbour. It is wonderful to have seen the seagulls soar and to still hear the ocean roar."

Author's note:

The seagulls have left the area in Seal Harbour where Gary grew up, since the fish heads and other tasty morsels (which were so plentiful when the fish plant was in operation) are no longer available.

Bethany, who lives in Vancouver, recalls that Gary's parents were quiet, gentle and humble people. Carrie, Gary's mother, was very fond of Bethany and enjoyed Bethany's visits in the summer. Bethany did not grow up in Seal Harbour but her mother Kay, a bit older than Gary, was brought up there. However, Bethany goes to the reunions when she can and was very close to her grandmother, who recently passed away, leaving a vacant homestead and lots of precious memories.

Gary had this to say about his parents:

"Dad was a man of few words and he seldom said the word no. So, while working 6 days a week at the two man, Seal Harbour fish plant, he didn't say 'no' to thirty-six years of service as the church treasurer. He was Credit Union President, Sunday School Superintendent, School Trustee, and County Councillor. He often canvassed for such causes as the Canadian Bible Society. Bedford Pinkham, who worked with Dad many decades ago, used to tell Charles and me that no matter what we might ever do, we would never be *half* the man our father was.

Mom was rather involved in community life as well. She was a teacher in our Sunday School, an active member of the Women's Missionary Society, a member of the Women's Institute of Nova Scotia and a member of the Ladies' Aid. When I was in grades 6, 7, and 8, she was also our Seal Harbour School teacher. You can rightly believe that I didn't get away with anything at school then. Mom always arranged for me to have a front seat in school. I always thought it was because of my bad behaviour but now I think that she knew I would have a better chance of hearing what was being taught."

Gary, Mom, Dad, and Charles

Proverbs 22:6 "Train a child in the way that he should go and when he is old he will not turn from it."

What a wonderful example Gary's parents were to him while he was growing up. Truly 'the acorn does not fall far from the tree'. It was fortunate for Gary that he was born to Christian parents with good work ethics. They obviously took their responsibility (to teach and equip Gary for life) seriously.

Presumably, it would have been a comfort for Gary to have his mother nearby, as he was bullied and made fun of on the school grounds. However, Gary tells me that it never seemed to occur to him to tell anyone what was going on because he would have felt like he was 'telling on' someone and you just didn't do that. It stands out as a very comforting memory of Gary's that Parker Langley stood up for him one time by getting angry at the other kids. At the very first reunion, Gary thanked Parker and asked him if he remembered the incident. Parker confirmed that he did indeed remember and they both said they could go to the school yard and point out where they were standing that day, perhaps 30 years earlier.

Gary hung out with another child named Alden whose mother was also a teacher. Alden had learning challenges of his own that were not well understood at the time. So, the two boys found some comfort in their mutual friendship. I have heard from Bethany Keddy, that part of the great admiration she has for Gary is because of the love and kindness he always bestowed upon Alden.

Buddies for Life - Alden and Gary

Gary tells the story of how, on his very first day of school, when the bell rang for recess, he mistakenly and anxiously ran out the door - up over the hill and all the way home.

The Seal Harbour School

Because of Gary's hearing challenge, he could not pronounce words properly. This was often interpreted as slowness on his part, which was far from the case. Fortunately, somehow, in spite of limited financial resources, Gary's family was able to make regular trips to Halifax (300 kilometers away) for speech therapy. It must have been a lot of hard work for Gary to practice the exercises to improve his speech and although he still had speech problems when he started Acadia University, the disciplines he learned then, helped him through. Gary is a wonderful record keeper and recently came across a notebook that he used to practice making sounds.

Many children have problems learning to use certain sounds in their speech, such as R, L, and the 'th' sound. Because of Gary's hearing challenge it was a real struggle for him to pronounce a lot of sounds. We learn to speak by hearing others, but if we can't hear the sounds well, a lot of letters get scrambled.

To help with the 'th' sound Gary had to practice by putting the tongue between the teeth and blowing gently th, th, th, and then practice putting the vowel sounds in front like a-th, i-th, o-th, ee-th, ay-th and oo-th. Can you imagine the discipline it would take for a young boy to make these sounds over and over again?

The "f" sound was particularly difficult and one exercise required counting from 50 – 59. The "f" sound is made by biting the lower lip gently and blowing gently. It would have been fun for us to recite this poem which many of us will remember from childhood. It would have been a major feat for Gary.

One, two, three, four, five - Once I caught a fish alive.
Six, seven, eight, nine, ten - Then I let him go again.
Why did you let him go? - Because he bit my finger so.
Which finger did he bite? - The little finger on the right.

The letter "S" was a difficult sound as well. Gary was told, "Put your teeth together and smile, as you blow through your teeth."

Stand up Stanley. Stand up Straight.
Stand up by the garden gate.
Stand up Stanley. Stand and stay.
Stop the mailman on his way.

Sharing His Great Love

Like Gary, I also still remember the following poem for mastering the letter "s" and have always liked it although I don't remember the occasion of hearing or reading it. It would have had greater meaning to Gary as it helped him master part of his speech problem.

Seven, sweet, singing birds, singing in a tree
Seven, swift, sailing ships, sailing out to sea
Seven, round rainbows, shining in the sun,
Seven, slim, race horses, steady for the run
Seven, silver butterflies, gleaming overhead
Seven, red roses, in a garden bed

So you can see the contrast between those of us who learned to speak the natural way by listening to parents and siblings and Gary who had to learn each sound the hard way with disciplined repetitions. Can you imagine a child who could not speak properly having aspirations to be a minister? It is a wonder to me that even if negative thoughts in his own mind didn't deter him, one of his family members, friends or peers didn't steal his dream.

One day Gary was walking along the swampy road by the fish plant where some men were working on the road. He suddenly realised that he could hear frogs peeping, which was something that he had only heard others speaking about. He blurted out, "I just heard some togs in the bog." Later that evening, when Gary stopped in to Harry's store, he found one of the men laughing heartily with the customers. There was no doubt in Gary's mind what caused the laughter when the man turned to Gary and said, "Oh, here comes old

'Togs in the Bog' now." Gary was devastated. For years after that many people knew him simply as 'Togs in the Bog'. Tears welled up in Gary's eyes as he recalled that incident. It was as if he were re-living all of the gut-wrenching feelings of that particular day in his youth.

It is really ironic that this small boy, teased so much by peers and adults alike, has been called back home to preside at many of their funerals. The Lord has restored to Gary some of the respect that the community had taken away.

Please do not miss the lesson here. As kids we used to be told, "Sticks and stones may break my bones, but names will never hurt me." However, somehow, even as we chanted that to the top of our lungs, deep down we wondered why it didn't seem true to us. It isn't true! The bruise from a stone will eventually go away but a couple of unkind words or an action can scar for a lifetime.

My husband Lloyd tells me of a time when his younger brother had a new pair of red rubber boots. He was so happy and proud of them. When an aunt came to visit he said, "Auntie, look at my new boots." She laughed, bent down and scooping up a bit of gravel, put it in his boot. Did she mean permanent harm? Probably not, but from then on he never liked that aunt even when he was a grown man and as you can see, the story continues to be told.

Perhaps today, the reason we appear to have so much bullying in our schools and on the internet is that because for so long, physical abuse got punished but emotional abuse never did. Nothing we say or do is insignificant, so perhaps we should make an effort to always leave a person better off for having interacted with us.

Gary's great sensitivity toward others is due in part to Biblical truths that spoke to him with relevance at an early stage in his life. I think we can all relate to this next story that Gary tells of childhood relationship issues gone badly and in retrospect taught Gary a lesson about what he wished on other people.

"I recall an incident when I was 7 or 8 years old. Marilyn Manthorne and I were in her family playhouse, which was one half of her grandfather George's shed by his back door. The other half was normally a wood shed. We were apparently 'on the outs' with Danny Willett and June Manthorne that day. I was painting some child-sized chairs and then sat down to philosophise about life - saying, 'I would laugh if Danny and June came along and sat down on the wet paint', whereupon, I jumped to my feet, realising it was I who had sat on the fresh green paint. I was wearing my brand new blue jeans. Mom cut the green swabs out of them and patched them up, making me literally the butt of my own judgemental attitudes toward our friends."

CHAPTER TWO

The Beginning of "The Call"

Psalm 119:11 "In my heart I store up your words, so I might not sin against you."

When Gary was 7 years old he requested a Bible of his own, which he received that Christmas in 1952, with an inscription from his grandmother (his father's mother). It was a black New Testament. Gary lovingly jokes that at the time, "They couldn't come up with the whole Bible." His grandmother died soon after, leaving the family very concerned about his aging grandfather. They wanted to make sure he was safe from evening until morning so somehow Gary was chosen to stay with him. They need not have worried, as the aging grandfather lived another sixteen years. Gary would go to his grandfather's every evening after the chores at home were done. His grandfather was a man of very few words but his example spoke volumes to Gary's young mind.

It is evident to me that children benefit from role models and roots to generations of people who are willing to be good role models for them. It is further evident that children need to be busy. Today, kids have so much time on their hands that they often complain that they are bored. Gary had no time for boredom when he was a child or when he was at Acadia University, as necessity kept him busy to pay his tuition.

One morning, as they were heading out of the cove to their lobster traps, Gary paused from rowing to grab a tissue out of his shirt pocket. A look of shock came over his grandfather's face until he realised Gary was blowing his nose. He said, "For a minute I thought you were reaching for a cigarette. I was going to drop you overboard if you had been." That kept Gary from smoking for a few years until he got to Acadia Greek Class, where (as students) they would join the professor in studiously smoking their pipes.

Every evening, Gary's grandfather would sit in his rocking chair and read a chapter of the Bible, dwelling on his favourite verses. Gary would do the same as he took out his little New Testament and sat beside him in his grandmother's rocking chair. It was there that Gary developed the habit of reading the 'word' and memorising favourite verses. Gary really liked John 3:16. "For this is the way God loved the world: He gave his one and only Son that everyone who believes in him should not perish but have eternal life." It meant so much to him that he had started to write a sermon on it when he was only 9 or 10 years old. As he grew older, Romans chapter 8 took on a very personal meaning to Gary and the wonderful instructions in Philippians, particularly chapter 4:8 "Whatever is true, whatever is worthy of respect, whatever is just, whatever is pure, whatever is lovely, whatever is commendable, if something is excellent or praiseworthy, think about these things."

Lessons from the Rocking Chair

Obviously God had his protective eye on Gary while he was growing up. Gary tells a story of the time he went hunting alone. He had bought a deer hunting license one fall and after school this particular day, he took his dad's 32 Winchester Special. Toting his weapon and no doubt a lunch, he climbed into a tree as was the custom of the day. On his way up the tree he heard a shot ring out and he thought someone was shooting at him. Due to his hearing problem he could not tell from which direction the shot was coming, nor how close the perpetrator was. He kept very still and moved quietly to his position in the tree. It was then that he noticed that the safety on his gun was off and it was his own gun that had fired the shot. Gary quips, "I guess that is what the Bible means by 'Judge not, that you be not judged'."

Gary was eleven years old when his father bought their very first car. Prior to that, they had walked everywhere, including to and from church. When Gary was old enough to get a driver's licence, Gary's father decided to use that as a bargaining tool to convince Gary to get rid of his popular Beatle's hair style - that was, in his father's opinion, too long. Gary wasn't quite ready for that and tried to reason with his father by arguing that Jesus had long hair. His father said, "Yes, you are correct, Jesus did have long hair and he also walked everywhere, didn't he?" Losing that argument, postponed Gary's chance for learning to drive for a while.

In Gary's own words, following is a humorous story of a boat and rebellion that didn't work out too well:

"Everyone in Seal Harbour has heard me tell the story of when I really got stranded. It was May 1960, perhaps the Victoria holiday. Al McFarland and I decided it was a good day to row to Goose Island, a 750 acre, special site a mile off shore. Both the fishermen at the fish plant and Dad, told us it wasn't a good day to do that, as it would be windy later. We thought, 'What do they know?' - when 90 year old George Manthorne's back was turned for a few minutes, we borrowed his skiff boat - a 'flat', and headed out to sea. After we landed on Goose Island, we spent the usual several hours combing the beach, circling the island until we came back where the boat was hauled ashore and, you guessed it, the wind had indeed come up and it was not safe to try to row home. Eventually, we saw a fishing boat approaching; Dad had asked Barney Langley to come rescue us. As another hymn put it, we had been "Drifting too Far From the Shore", by our own reckless choice.

I have mentioned this rescue to Barney different times over the years and have thanked him publicly. The last time I did so he said, 'I did it for your father. If it had been up to me, I would have left you there.' I thanked him one last time when I told that little story at his funeral in September, 1997."

The Shore

With his fetish for building, Gary also decided to build a boat. When it was time for the launching, Gary carefully pushed it into the water where it immediately took on water and promptly sank. Here is the story in Gary's own words:

"Cousins Brent and Warren Manthorne inherited their boat-building skills from their grandfather, Charlie O'Hara. Warren is presently building a 72 foot boat in Truro. While I was still a youngster at home, I decided to see if I had inherited any such skills. I set to work in private on the quiet shore of Long Cove near our house and eventually had a ten foot row boat ready to launch. As I pushed it out from shore, I jumped in. As it glided out into deeper water, the boat sank on its maiden voyage, with me still in it but without the maiden. Perhaps that's why I appreciated the words from a hymn I ran across a few years later, 'I was Sinking deep in Sin, Far from the Peaceful Shore'."

However, Gary's skill in driving a nail would serve him well in the years to come when he would build his own Valley home, a place he could live for most of his ministry years. Gary's carpenter skills came into play later in life too when he found himself without a church ministry, at a low spot in his life.

Here are some reflections from Gary's brother Charles on growing up with Gary:

"Gary is three years younger than me; thus, growing up we were a bit separated in interests. I do recall how I would at times argue with our mother that I did not want to take Gary along, and we did have separate friends who were more our individual ages. Our paternal grandmother died suddenly on a Sunday afternoon in 1955 from I believe - an aneurism, leaving our grandfather alone. I was 13 years of age and Gary was 10. Sometime after Grandmother's death, Gary was 'appointed', he says, to spend the nights with Grandfather. That created a bit of a separation between us for a time. From an early age, Gary had a speech and hearing issue which probably received serious attention only after he arrived in Wolfville to attend Acadia. The hearing and speech matter probably was an embarrassment to me as a kid so thus my 'reluctance to take Gary along', to quote our late mother. Being a kid in Seal Harbour in the 50's without the toys kids of today have, was centered around the one room schoolhouse, the church, the grocery store, the rural post office and the 'cove'. The cove was a bit of a sand beach where the fishing boats were kept. The fish plant, where our father worked, was there and the men had fish stores where they mended their fishing gear and told stories. Some of the stories may have even been true. We stood for each other when we were married, me in 1964 and Gary in 1968, I believe.

Along with Gloria, my later to be wife, I drove Gary from Halifax to Acadia University on the eve of his starting studies at Acadia. By previous plan - (I don't know whose plan), we picked up a spinster school teacher in Windsor. Ruth Speight was a friend of our uncle who was a fundamentalist Baptist Minister. I think she was a plant to ensure the arrival went as it should.

After arrival at Acadia we met another new student, Don Cameron, Gary's assigned room-mate, who became a friend of Gary's during his time at Acadia. Gary complained of having a bit of a cold that night. Don replied, "We'll go downtown and find something to cure the cold." Ruth, the school teacher, immediately went on alert that Don was perhaps dragging Gary off to the tavern to fix the cold.

Our contact has been more so in our adult life than as kids, which may seem strange, but three years age difference as an adult seems not as great as three years as a child. Gary has a great interest in our roots and the way 'it used to be', this referring to people and events of our childhood. You may know by experience that Gary has a great interest in people and events; remembering events and dates of years ago, while forgetting at times what he did yesterday. He probably remembers whose funeral he conducted in 1982 along with the weather at the time, connecting an ancestor of the deceased to a funeral of someone he will conduct in *2012.*"

Author's Note:

Ruth Speight was one of my teachers at Duncan Macmillan High School in Sheet Harbour. She no doubt followed Gary's uncle 'Down East' but I learned only recently of her habit of following him around. She kept it a secret and joined the choir at our United Church, some miles from where Gary's uncle was ministering. I got to sit next to her. She was a robust, tall lady with reddish hair and freckles and if I had to guess I would say, German decent. She often drew smiles from the other sopranos with her powerful voice. Miss Speight felt that it was her duty to watch over me as well. My boyfriend and I were the recipients of many of her 'little talks'. One of her favourites was that we should not under any circumstance be un-chaperoned.

I also knew Gary's uncle, the Baptist minister, but if Ruth ever mentioned him, I never got the connection between the two of them. Gary and I have had a few laughs over this but all-in-all, Ruth was a good influence on me. It would benefit kids today to have such an iron-fisted teacher who really cared about whether or not they messed up. Later on, I discovered that Ruth Speight also taught Dr. Harry Gardner in grade 10. When I visited Dr. Gardner at Acadia University, we shared some pleasant memories of her.

Reflections from Rev. John Beers, one of the pastors who visited the Manthorne family while Gary was still at home in Seal Harbour:

"1963 stands out as a very significant year in world history and for me personally. It was the year that President John F. Kennedy was assassinated and a week later my father died. In the midst of all that was taking place, I was very fortunate to have been placed as a summer student on the Isaac Harbour, Country Harbour and Goshen, pastorate. It was during this summer that I had the pleasure of meeting the Manthorne family of which Gary was one of two sons.

Although the Manthorne family lived across the Harbour from where I served as a pastor, they would occasionally attend special services being held where I ministered. Being the hospitable people that they were, they invited me on several occasions to join them for a meal. During one of the visits at their home, a discussion took place as to what the next steps would be for Gary in terms of further studies and/or work. He had just graduated from High School and was searching for a career direction. During the discussion I asked Gary if he had ever considered attending Acadia University with the thought of studying for the ministry.

This lead to a discussion of the pros verses cons of making such a decision. At that time, there was a thread of uncertainty as to what Gary felt his future would hold for him.

I believe at that point, I asked Gary if it might be a good idea to consider Acadia University for his first degree and during that time become familiar with the School of Theology and what that department had to offer. Also, I suggested that there were Christian organizations on the campus that could be beneficial to the process of making a decision as to whether or not the ministry would be a meaningful vocation for him.

From that summer until the present, we have been good friends. Such friendship was enhanced by my having ministered in neighbouring pastorates, sharing ministry experiences during my years as Area Minister, as well as meeting at many varied church and community events. It seems appropriate to mention here, Dr. Millard R. Cherry, a mutual friend and mentor. He, like Barnabas in the Bible, was an encourager, filled with the Holy Spirit and faith and as such, he influenced and inspired both of us as we worked through the call of God on our lives, for Christian Ministry.

As a result of my life having intercepted with Gary's, my contribution to his call of God to the Christian ministry has been minimal; in terms of the benefits of friendship - I will be forever grateful."

Author's notes on meeting John Beers and his wife Ethel:

During 2007/2008, my husband Lloyd and I were attending a Bible study at the home of the Rev. Sterling Gosman, and his wife Anne. It was a small cell group of the New Minas Baptist Church where we later became church members. We had met Sterling and Anne about 12 years before while facilitating meetings with a Dietary Supplement Company in the Truro area. They are the parents of the great Canadian soprano, Measha Brueggergosman. We knew them to be wonderful Christian people and we had stayed overnight with them at their home in Fredericton, New Brunswick, while we were en route to the United States.

The morning we left, Sterling prayed for us and specifically that God's angels would surround the car on the trip; not only around the car but under the car. Once on our way, I questioned aloud why he would pray for angels under the car. The next evening at dusk, it became evident as a blinding sunset obscured Lloyd's view.

We missed our stop and needed to turn around quickly. In a flash our car was suspended on a median between two busy roads. For a few seconds, we didn't know what to do and then I told Lloyd that when I gave him the 'all clear' signal he should step on the gas and see what happened. I was sure the whole bottom would fall out of the car. When I gave the signal, and Lloyd stepped on the gas, that car literally floated up and off the median as if giant hands had lifted it and placed it down on the road, facing in the right direction. I looked at Lloyd in that instance and exclaimed, "Angels under the car!"

We had little contact with the Gosmans after that. Our lives were very busy and Sterling and Anne had made some major changes. They had sold their Fredericton house and moved to Wolfville - where Sterling had attended Acadia University.

Lloyd and I had moved to the Valley several years before that.

Lloyd had always been fond of Sterling; me, sometimes not so much. I always found him to be a bit narrow in his views where women were concerned, especially strong, opinionated women. Those who know me well will get the significance of that. In later years I came to respect him for his wonderful pastoral qualities and I would say we've both matured and we're 'good'. Lloyd heard that Sterling had graduated and had accepted a position as Minister of Visitation for the New Minas Baptist Church. He decided that, in honour of Sterling's accomplishment, we should take Sterling and Anne to the Old Orchard Inn for dinner. We got caught up on a lot of years in the conversation. It was there that we found out that Sterling was leading the 'small group' Bible study in his home and Lloyd asked if we could attend. I guess that Sterling could not turn him down.

Now back to John and Ethel Beers:

We attended Bible Study and in December we had a Christmas Party. I was not aware that John and Ethel were a part of that Bible study until they showed up at that party. I found out that John was filling in and trouble-shooting for Calvary Baptist Church in Spryfield, so they were living in Halifax temporarily. The church had recently had a split in their congregation and John was known for his ability to help get things back on track and help heal the 'wounds' of separation.

Lloyd and I had bought a condo in Halifax and were spending a lot of time there in the winter, so I told John we would visit his church some Sunday.

We did visit and found that it was the church that Rev. Owen Cockrane and his daughter Ann attended. They are distant relatives of ours and I had played the organ for special services in the West Brooklyn Church where Barb, another daughter of Owen's, was pastor. We had also met them all at the summer services in the Sherwood Church where we all had roots. Lloyd and I continued at the Calvary Baptist Church as visitors and supported them whenever we could. I filled in on the piano a couple of times, sang in the choir and we contributed financially to the church as well. It was at a New Year's Eve party at the Manse where John and Ethel were living that we really got to know the 'jovial' John and the 'competitive' Ethel, as we took pictures, played games and rang in the New Year. It was also then that I learned that Ethel was a sister to Lawson Aulenback, whom we had met when he was the leader of the Somerset Hymn Sing. He had become ill and I had been praying for him for a long time. Unfortunately he has since passed away.

In 2009, I received a call informing me that the church Pastor and also the organist at the Forest Hill Baptist Church had resigned and they wanted me to come and play the organ. I think that I agreed to help them temporarily and I am still there. That was when they called Gary Manthorne as their pastor. In 2011, the church had a huge celebration for Gary's 41 years in the Ministry. I played the organ for that service and was there that I learned of John's connection to Gary. As this book goes to print, I find myself once again working with Rev. John Beers – this time at the Cambridge Baptist Church where John is Interim Pastor and I am the organist for the summer months of 2013. This seems to further substantiate how we are all connected to one another.

CHAPTER THREE
Tales from Acadia University Days

Gary tells me that two other Seal Harbour High School alumni, Glen Manthorne and Joyce Manthorne, had already graduated from Acadia by the time he showed up in his black leather jacket and rubber boots. His take on his first term at Acadia follows, and a letter from home reveals a very wise and loving father.

"My first term at Acadia threatened to become my last. Though my marks in High school just barely got me into Acadia, nonetheless I wasn't used to failing tests or exams. When I flunked a midterm within my first six weeks, I took it as a sign that I wasn't University material after all.

Apparently, I wrote home and said I was about to quit. I had written to Mom and Dad weekly throughout my Acadia years and Mom wrote weekly as well. This was a custom we kept going until Mom became unable to write in the mid 1980's. Once in a while Dad would write a letter back. The most important letter I ever got was dated Seal Harbour, October 30, Wed. 7 PM. Here it is, just the way Dad wrote it."

"Dear Gary,

It is always good to get your letters and to know how you are getting along. We were glad to get your letter today. I am sure you had a good trip to Sydney and it would be a good experience - of course it would be a very tiresome trip. You mentioned that you are a bit discouraged over one of your tests recently. No matter what one is doing, there is always discouraging times. If it was not for the dark clouds, the sunshine would not seem so bright. I feel sure that you realise you have a great opportunity to get somewhere in this life if you are willing to try. We know that you are trying and we are not thinking that you will not make out ok. You can do it and we know you will............."

The reader can see from this letter that Gary's father was a great encourager. Also, it must have been instilled in Gary that a close family connection is important. As well, there is the discipline of consistently sending letters back and forth. I am sure that some of us didn't have this same experience when we left home for the first time. Gary's father and mother spoke positive words to him and their confidence in him sustained him and helped him get over his first disappointment at Acadia University.

It is never too early to speak words of blessing over our children. I remember praying over my children when they were just babies in the crib, asking God to 'walk' with them and to give them favour during their lives. I didn't know then, just how much that would mean to them for the journey they would have to face.

Sharing His Great Love

People of all ages suffer from low self-esteem. Many successful people have become successful because when they could not believe in themselves, others believed in them. That knowledge alone shows the power that we can have in this world.

After his first student pastorate, in Charlotte County N.B. in the summer of 1965, Gary came home for a few days before starting a new term at Acadia. He decided to have one last sleep-over in his camp before heading back. He had built his camp over the years from scraps of anything he could find which included discarded pieces of wood, trees and cardboard. It was a shelter from the elements and a real attraction to the cousins who came to visit. They loved to get away to Gary's camp which was not far from the house. On Labour Day in 1965 Gary nearly burned down the family home when the beloved cabin he had been building over his teen years in the woods near the house, burned to the ground. With Gary's hearing problem he was a sound sleeper and was not immediately aware of the commotion. He and his best friend Alden thankfully escaped the fire and read about it on the front page of the Canso Breeze Weekly a few days later. Gary says, "My brother Charles did better with fires. He had the responsible job of making the fires in the school house for $35 a year."

Gary noted that his proclivity towards fires stayed with him at Acadia as well, when smoke was seen coming from under his room door into the hallway. He had plugged in his jiffy jug to make coffee and then decided to go downtown to the Post Office leaving the jiffy jug still turned on and forgotten about. When he arrived back, the neighbours in his hallway said they had just broken into his room to rescue him and fellow student, Dale Hennigar, was going back down the hall with the fire extinguisher. Dale is now a retired High School Principal.

Selwyn Hopkins, who later became a military chaplain, was Gary's best buddy and roommate for part of the time he was at Acadia. He was nicknamed 'Hopper' because of his athletic abilities and they enjoyed bouncing the basketball around at times. One Sunday night they decided to skip Chapel and hang out with the Varsity guys in the gym. They had to break in because the gym was locked. There was no-one there. The next day they found out that all of the Varsity guys had gone to Chapel. Gary recently visited Selwyn Hopkins on a visit to Ontario.

Gary and Selwyn

Sharing His Great Love

Gary says that he had no detectible athletic skills, so he was very proud when he broke his foot playing basketball with the fellows who were visiting from the Moncton Bible School. When asked what happened he would proudly say, "Oh, I broke my foot playing basketball against the team from Moncton."

In addition to University Chapel twice a day Monday to Friday, there was also Theology Chapel once or twice a week at Sawyer Hall. In their graduating year each student would take a turn as speaker of the week. Gary remembers the last Theology Chapel as it was ending. He felt very sentimental and teary eyed, realising that he had been blessed with a wonderful experience to have been at Acadia for those seven years and that it was about to conclude. He realised that he had been in a somewhat insulated environment and that soon he would depart for the real world.

Gary reflects, "Imagine being in classes with Dr. Cherry! (Dr. Cherry's bio is at the back of the book). Imagine being involved with Charles Taylor, the author of Canada's Clinical Training, as he nurtured us for Hospital, Prison and Pastoral Ministry. Charlie forced us to look deep into our own minds and hearts to deal with and heal from old wounds and blind spots. In the mid 1950's, Charlie had sat at our dinner table in Seal Harbour when he brought the renowned Acadia Quartet to our church. He became a part of the nurturing that sent me on to Acadia years later."

Author's note:

In the 1970's, while I was involved in the prison ministry in Saint John, New Brunswick, I heard

Charlie Taylor speak and purchased his book "Only Love Heals." The price on the inside cover is $2. It has always had a prominent place in our home where visitors could pick it up to read, and this is still true today.

Fredericton's Dr. Alison Trites arrived at Acadia as New Testament Professor. He and his wife Gene became Gary's friends for life. Their two boys, Jonathan and Ian, would come over to babysit the Manthornes' slightly younger boys, Alan and Andrew. In the 1980's, Alison and Gary would help each other out with chores at their respective cabins. The Trites were at Sunken Lake and the Manthornes were at Avonport Beach.

At one point, Alison was even doing some work at Gary's house and offered to pile the wood. Gary says, "Apparently he had not bothered to show up for the wood stacking lecture when he was taking his PHD because a couple of nights later the Manthornes were awakened by a thunderous racket in the basement when Alison's 'neatly piled' stack of wood came crashing to the floor. I remembered how he would generously give me a B- in a New Testament paper and I realised the best I could do for him would be to give him an F in wood stacking."

I met with Dr. Trites and his wife Gene to see if he would like to defend himself on the wood stacking story. He remembered doing the stacking but didn't think he ever knew that the pile fell over. Oops! It's out now.

Dr. Trites was Dean of Residence at the School of Theology and in particular he spoke of Eaton House. He told me that Gary was mostly responsible for the 'fun' at Eaton House. I didn't ask his definition of fun but I was thinking Shenanigans.

Linda Manthorne, Gary's first wife, and Gene Trites were good friends and they were both teachers. They devised a plan where the two guys would work together on some projects. They proposed the idea to Alison and Gary who seemed to think it was a good plan. Alison wanted a small shed and Gary, being the skilled carpenter of the two, told him he could have a 12x12 shed for the price of a smaller one. Alison told Gary, "I can drive a nail, carry, and pass things to you." So the shed, which has stood the test of time, became a proud reality.

Alison did other chores for Gary like piling boulders and tree stumps around the water line of the Manthorne cottage to protect the property. He says of his time working with Gary, "These were some of the best times of my life. I think it was a delight to both of us." Both Alison and Gene spoke lovingly of Gary, and Gene compared Gary's personality to that of the late, gentle Rita McNeill whose funeral was taking place that very day on April 22, 2013.

The Trites also spoke of Gary's great kindness to Dr. Cherry. While everyone's beloved 'Cherry' was in his last days in the hospital, they said it was Gary who held things together for them all. Dr. Cherry was never left alone.

I also discussed the late Rev. Glen Lidstone with Dr. Trites. Glen was a friend of Gary's and an acquaintance of mine. Dr. Trites told me that Glen was his very best student and he expressed sadness in his tragic passing. I asked what kind of student Gary Manthorne was and he said, "I can tell you that there is a great deal more intelligence there than you might think." I just smiled and I didn't ask him *what* he thought I might think.

CHAPTER FOUR

The Circuit Ridin' Preacher Begins his Ministry

Two years before Gary graduated from Acadia, the Greenfield churches where he had served as a student in 1966, invited him back as their regular minister. Linda became involved in the Middlefield Church with the Sunday school and she initiated a Pathfinders group for all of the churches. The small Middlefield Church congregation included a devoted mother and son. Gary says, "The Lord was already at work in Harry Gardener's life when he approached me for baptism. It was indeed a privilege to baptise him and his lifelong friend and neighbour, Carol Dunn, at the Long Lake Youth Camp."

The Harry Gardner of whom Gary speaks, has served as Executive Minister of the Atlantic Baptist Convention for several years and now is the principal of the Acadia Divinity College. He is also widely known in international church circles. Carol too, heard the call to the ministry and has been serving in Maritime churches. Gary quips, "They were my first baptisms; thankfully, they survived my inexperience and many have been blessed by them."

I agree with Gary that many have been blessed by them. It reminds me of the saying, "You can count the seeds in an apple, but you cannot count the apples in one seed." God calls us all to plant the seeds, and to rely on his promise to produce the harvest. Gary, from my prospective, is a seed planter who has full trust in the partnership with God. He doesn't spend time worrying about whether the seed will take root and grow. You don't put seeds in the ground and then watch and worry over which ones will come up. You just plant and water and trust that since they came up before and you got the harvest, they will come up again. You just keep planting. You just keep on believing.

Gary says, "After I scraped through the Convention Examining Council for Ordination, I proceeded with the plans for the ordination at the Greenfield Church," Dr. Cherry was the speaker at the special service and there was painting being done in advance that kept getting delayed. The service had to be shifted to the Fire Hall. This seemed appropriate to Gary considering the many 'fiery' escapades he had experienced along with the fact that he and some kids had taken the fire truck to a woods fire while most of the regular firemen were working in town.

I have often heard comments that it is unusual that most of Gary's ministry has been in the Annapolis Valley. It is quite unusual but most understandable to me. When we are young we are most impressionable. Both Gary and I fell in love with the Annapolis Valley when we were quite young.

My best friend for many years was Sharon Green. My brother Carroll was named after her father, Dr. Carroll Green. Another of my brothers was named after Sheldon Green, Dr. Green's brother. The Greens were from the Valley (I believe the Pereaux area) but both had lived in Sheet Harbour. Sheldon had been the manager at the bank and Carroll had been our doctor and next-door neighbor. Obviously, both of them had made favourable impressions upon my parents, Howard and Bernice Spears.

Dr. Green was married to Phyllis who was a Westcott. Her home in the Valley is now the site of the lovely Benjamin Ridge Winery, on the White Rock Road. Grandmother Wescott often visited the Greens in Sheet Harbour. I would listen in amazement to the stories the family would tell about the Annapolis Valley and the beautiful apple blossoms. As a child, I planted many apple seeds, hoping to grow my very own orchard - but I only grew weeds. It was always my unspoken wish to visit the Valley and destiny landed me here 16 years ago.

When Gary was a young boy he found a book called "A Tale of Old Acadia", which was an historical fiction story of Acadia College in its early years, around 1850. He didn't ask but it might have been a gift from his mother to his father as she had written his father's name in it. Gary enjoyed the book so much that he read it several times. The story fascinated him and he fell in love with the Annapolis Valley and with Acadia.

When Gary was 15, he went to Wolfville with Rev. Rob Currie and his wife Joan, to attend his very first Baptist Youth Convention. He was thrilled to see the names of places (from the book that he had read) popping up on the road signs - Grand

Pre - Melanson - Gaspereau - Minas Basin - The Ridge - Wolfville and Acadia. For the first time in his life, the written word was coming to life for Gary. It felt magical, like a dream come true. Gary says, "That fascination has never left me. As a result, it was so exciting for me to become a student at Acadia and to spend most of my life since then in this very same beautiful landscape that I had read about in my childhood."

Here are Gary's reflections on leaving the Greenfield Pastorate and his memories of the other Pastorates which formed a circuit of his ministry, most (except for Clarence and Seal Harbour) within 40 kilometers of the house he built in Melanson.

"I remember driving away after my last service in Greenfield, heading for the Gaspereau Parsonage. Linda had left earlier in her Volkswagen Bug. Her car was jammed packed and I had a sofa attached to the roof of my Bug. I remember second-guessing the decision to move back to the Valley, and was tearfully asking myself, 'Why are we leaving this wonderful place?' I have been back many times over the years for different invitations, including the dedication of their new church in August 1984, when they gave me the honor of 'preaching it open'.

Greenfield was also a great territory because of its miles of beautiful Ponhook Lake shore. After

Linda and I and our two miniature Dachsunds moved to the Gaspereau Valley in the fall of 1972, we missed Greenfield so much that we kept going back for part of our summer vacations.

One of the first couples I married, our good friends Garry and Dianne Simpson, sold us (or practically GAVE us) a piece of their shoreline, whereupon in 1976 I started building a cottage, helped along considerably by my good Melanson buddy Alex Smith and also Dad who was able to help us because he had just retired from the Fish Plant back home. As a family, we had some great summers at the cottage and on the lake but after a while we found it challenging to get away from the Valley for long enough. We ended up selling it and buying an old run down cabin at Avonport Beach in 1983. I spent any spare time in the summers 'til 1988 renovating it, but by that time we had lost our enthusiasm for cottage life. The family home that I had built in Melanson on a large wooded lot was more of a get-a-way spot than the cabin on the tiny lot.

All of this building felt like a reflection of my mother's heritage because all of her brothers were carpenters, except for George who was a Baptist Minister. Thankfully, the two cabins and the family home were great improvements over the fire trap I had built as a kid in Seal Harbour. Eventually one CAN learn from experience.

The One that burned,

Looking Better

Sharing His Great Love

The Masterpiece

CHAPTER FIVE

The Circuit Ridin' Preacher in the Gaspereau Valley

1972 to 1977

"We took up residence in the Gaspereau Parsonage in September 1972. We had two, miniature Dachshunds named Oscar and Heidi. After carefully studying their athletic ability and how high they could jump, I built them an outside pen around two sides of the parsonage, very nicely and neatly done. I put the dogs in their pen to let them get acquainted with it and Linda and I took a walk down the road past the Coldwell's. We didn't get very far before we realised the dogs had jumped the fence and were walking along with us. I then had to build an awkward looking 6 inch extension to the height of the pen, which ruined my original artistic design.

When our older son Allan was old enough to enjoy playing outside, I built a lovely, red fence directly accessible through the back door. So, there we were enjoying it together. I ducked into the house for a minute and when I came back out, yes, you guessed it! He was gone. He had crawled up on the cellar hatches and jumped HIS fence. It was a frantic half hour till we found him wandering around the field behind Ralph Gertridge's place.

Allan's birth was the personal highlight of those years. He arrived on May 30, 1975. I took Linda to the hospital in Wolfville at 9:00PM and he was born just after midnight. When I phoned Linda's parents in Vancouver, they got the exciting news of their first grandson while for them it was still May 29. I went home and stayed up to celebrated with Hank Williams songs all night.

At 5.30AM, knowing that Alex would be getting up for work in Halifax, I stood singing under the bedroom window of Alex and Cheryl Smith, proudly announcing the birth. Alex always says I woke them up meowing like a cat and then burst forth into Johnny Cash's song "I Walk the Line". With the light of a new day now underway in Eastern Canada, it would soon be time to phone my mom and dad in Seal Harbour.

In addition to the regular three Sunday services of White Rock, Gaspereau, and Wallbrook, I met with the Men's Group and Youth Groups in White Rock and Wallbrook. A lot of my time was spent in pastoral visitation in the Valley and up in the various mountain communities. I loved the communities, churches and people but went through a lot of self-doubt during those years, wondering if I should be doing something else. I even temporarily explored a possible Real Estate career at the same time that Bruce Rand of the Pereaux Church was likewise checking out an alternative career path. Bruce soon went back working on his farm, later becoming a very successful produce farmer who was eventually recognized as the 'Broccoli King'. Bruce was Chairman of the Board of Deacons at the Pereaux Church by the time I came there.

I did the four-week course in real estate and when Vaughan Henshaw shared the test results with me he said, 'I am afraid the results suggest you wouldn't do very well in real estate.' I think it might have had something to do with the possibility of me having so much empathy with both buyer and seller, that I would have a hard time negotiating the sale. In any case, it was a great relief, for I already knew in that short period of time that sales would never be part of my life. (Vaughan Henshaw, who was then in real estate, is now a Baptist Pastor).

It was mid-way through my Gaspereau Valley ministry years that Jim and John Allen lost their barn and cattle in a fire. It was deliberately set in the late night of the last Friday of June, 1975. The local people were very upset and felt great compassion for Eva, Jim and John. So, Harry How and I decided to invite everyone to get together at the Melanson Hall, where the decision was made by the crowd in attendance that we would build them a barn. We would start with going to the woods to cut logs the coming Saturday. Ivan Levy's mill crew volunteered their time to saw the lumber on their day off. Carey Brothers of Avonport donated the labor and material for the foundation. Then the community volunteers went to work evenings and Saturdays, through 'til November. In addition to all of the donation of labor and material, the public responded with cash donations, resulting in it costing the Allens only $150 for their new barn.

We were so wonderfully supported by the media – the local weekly paper ran a story on the project for weeks and ATV came to interview me about it. I seemed to be recognised as the spokesperson for the project but it was of course the hard work and generosity of a multitude of folks that made it a successful project that summer. Alex Smith made a sign for the roadside end of the barn that expresses the community sentiment with the words 'The Spirit of 1975'.

The ministry was going well and the people were so supportive. Nonetheless, I was restless and I could not shake the feeling that I wasn't doing it well. So, we finally decided I'd resign and I would 'try my hand' at carpentry for a while. We did know that we wanted to keep living in the Gaspereau Valley. After 3 months of working with Harold and Garth Hancock's fellows we took the plunge and I started building the family home on our lovely wooded lot that dear friends Basil and Ruby Smith had sold us at a generous discount. The foundation was contracted out to Perley Davidson and completed by Labor Day weekend at the end of August, 1977. I spent any spare time between then and June 24, 1978, working on the house.

The house-building project turned out to be another 'community spirit' project, with local fellows donating generous time and skills. It was post and beam construction, so at times I needed help lifting up the 20 foot, 4 by 12, Douglas Fir beams into place overhead. Cecil and Billy Reid gave me a hand with those. The roof was still open

Sharing His Great Love

into the first of December. The local fellows - Jim and John Allen, Basil Smith, Freeman Cross and Ray Ellis among them, declared a work party and spent Saturday boarding in the roof and tar-papering it. The next morning, Nova Scotia was covered with the first snow of the season!

I did all of the drywall by myself including carrying the heavy sheets up two flights of Stairs, but Clyde Forsythe then came over after his regular day's work and did the crack filling of the whole house. Laurie Levy followed in those generous footsteps and did all of the interior painting. Jim Harvey came along and helped me install many of the windows. In the meantime, the plumbing was getting started and eventually the kitchen cabinets. My best of friends, Alex Smith, did both of those major jobs from start to finish as another generous gift toward us getting established in our Melanson home. So, no wonder we love the Gaspereau Valley and its people! They have always been so wonderfully kind. So, when I say I built the family home - you can now see that the community actually built the house and donated it to us." Here are some reflections from Alex Smith of the Wallbrook Church, in the Gaspereau Valley:

"I first met Gary when he visited Wallbrook as part of a Gospel Team. He was also working with a boy's group in East Wolfville. During the summer of 1965, Gary took a student pastorate in New Brunswick. In 1982 I had the good fortune to accompany him when he re-visited the pastorate.

Each of us has a 'song to sing'. Gary Manthorne and Wilf Carter's origins were similar. They were both Guysborough boys who came to the Valley.

They both loved country music. Wilf began his career by learning to yodel in the parlours and apple orchards of Canning. Gary began his singing career in the church choirs and fields of the Gaspereau Valley. Of course Wilf went on to be Canada's yodelling cowboy and Gary went on to be Nova Scotia's Circuit Ridin' Preacher. Like Hank Snow, by now he's been 'everywhere'.

In the 1970's Gary had a piece of land on Ponhook Lake in Queen's County, so Gary and I pre-fabricated a frame for a cottage in the basement of the Gaspereau Church. Then we transported the materials to his site where we assembled the cottage. All went well until about 3:00PM when Gary informed me he had sliced his finger. We quickly headed off on a 50 mile round trip drive to the Lunenburg hospital. Gary got his finger stitched and on our return we continued our work.

I treasure my friendship with Gary and the many memories and talks we shared over coffee. Cheryl and I are most grateful for the times he has been there for us both as a pastor and a friend."

CHAPTER SIX

The Circuit Ridin' Preacher in Pereaux

October 1st, 1978 to July 31st, 1982.

"250 people showed up at the Induction Service in October to welcome me back into the Ministry. Pereaux was blessed with such wonderful leaders as Harriett and Emerson Thorpe, and among the many delightful homes and families, the large and ever-expanding Rand family. Some years later, in 1985, Harriett and Emerson came to Seal Harbour for our second annual reunion. As I welcomed them from the Pulpit to the morning service I said that we had a great arrangement while I was at Pereaux - Harriett and Emerson did all the work and I got the pay. Anyone associated with the Pereaux Church through the years, knows I wasn't really stretching that one much at all.

Pereaux was my first commuting experience since student days so I was always in their community; that is, away from home at noon-time. So, you know what that meant. I expanded my unsavory reputation of combining pastoral visitation with eating out. Twenty five years later I stopped in at Randall and Marion Lyon's house one day on a Valley visit from Guysborough County. No-one was home but I saw on the calendar that they had an appointment in Halifax. I figured that since it was noon, I'd make myself a lunch anyway and before I left I put a note on the table to tell them where the Mounties could find me for my break and enter. Sometimes people would ask me to tell them who was the best cook. Though I never excelled in my classes at Acadia, I was too smart to fall for THAT question. They were all the best, of course.

One morning, just after our younger son Andrew was born and Linda had gotten up in the night to feed him, I got up before daylight for his next feeding. I then decided I might as well stay up and head for Pereaux. There were no lights on in any houses until I got to Charles and Roberta Greene's in Blomidon, so of course I went in and helped make our breakfast. For years after that incident, Charlie would always say that I was the hardest working minister they ever had because I came to work every morning at 6:30AM. I think both he and I knew that he was exaggerating but hey, a fellow has to collect his positive references when they're offered so freely.

When I returned to the Pereaux Church 28 years later, in 2010, for a second round of ministry, this time with Mark Parent, Lois Melvin had progressed through the church hierarchy to the point of being my fashion advisor. Each Sunday, she would evaluate my clerical robes of the day, "That's a nice suit you have on today." One particular day, my integrity compelled me to confess that White's

Funeral Home had given it to me. While visiting in Toronto in September 2008, I received a phone call to do Clarke Vaughan's funeral in Kentville. I didn't have time to go back to Seal Harbour for my proper clothes, so I asked Cyril White if I could borrow a tie and jacket. Jim appeared with a suit, shirt, tie, and shoes that fit perfectly. When I was giving it all back to them the next day they said, "Oh, you can keep them." With a few other suits that Lois approved of, I sometimes had to confess, "Oh, a widow gave me this one after I had her husband's funeral." My expensive, selective and stylish taste in clothes was also demonstrated by the multi-colored, clip-on tie that seemed to go with anything. It shows up in pictures from 25 years ago and ever since.

As I write these words in April 2013, I have just concluded my second term of ministry at Pereaux. I am testing out what semi-retirement might feel like at 67. It was so good to be with the communities of Pereaux - Delhaven - Blomidon for two terms, a generation apart."

CHAPTER SEVEN
The Circuit Ridin' Preacher in Avonport - Lockhartville

August, 1982 to February, 1988

"As has been the case with some of the other churches where I have ministered, the Avonport part of the Avonport - Lockhartville pastorate was in low morale. Attendance and finances were suffering when they called me in 1982. With my usual approach of ignoring obvious issues, I made no mention of the problems and simply preached the 'Good News' and hung around with the people of the communities. The attendance and finances were soon no problem at all. I have always operated on the principle that if a minister is doing the job in a decent way, things work better if you are encouraging the congregation instead of nagging them.

I ran into a lot of 'bills' while in Avonport; thankfully not ones I had to pay - they were Bill Crosby, Bill Smith, Bill Coldwell and Bill Sweet. Both Bill Sweet and Bill Smith were terrible torments and kept me 'on my toes' wondering what twist they were going to put on anything I said or did. Bill Sweet and I had been on the same house-building project in Wolfville in the summer of 1977. One warm day, I had taken off my brand new Fireman's jacket and laid it on some building material. I forgot about it and went home without it. When I came back in the morning it was gone, along with my tape measure - only the Fire Department crests remained, having been torn off the jacket. Bill still teases me that he has a Fireman's jacket and a measuring tape at home.

After Bill Smith heard about the 1965 cabin fire, he never missed an opportunity to tease me in front of others by saying that I had burned the cabin down to collect the insurance to pay my way through Acadia. One of these days I will show him the newspaper article that concludes by saying that there was no insurance.

Just as I did in my other pastorates, I went to the office in Avonport every morning by 8:00AM and various fellows would stop in throughout the week to talk. My most frequent visitors were Avery Bird, Bill Crosby, Charlie Coldwell and the three giant Fuller brothers. It was a real privilege to talk with those guys.

Lockhartville Church completed two building projects during those years. The basic work was done by the people of the church. 'Dear Old' Dolly Schofield seemed like a mother to me and more-or- less adopted me into her (already sizable) family. She'd not only have me in for lunch but she would send me home with pies and other goodies. She would often say to me, 'Please don't ever leave this church while I am still alive because it would kill me to see you go'. So it was tough for both me and her when I eventually told her I was moving to the Aldershot Church. Sure enough, I came back for her funeral within a month of my leaving. Lockhartville's Stoney Hill Church was always a great site for Sunday evening Hymn Sings and the tradition still goes on today. Leading such an event was a new experience for me and I've enjoyed leading hundreds of these events over the years since. Notice that I said leading. Of course I was never the official, 'special musical guest', although once in a while, I'd cut loose with a song or hymn anyway - thanks to organists with a tolerance for spontaneity.

Avonport Church was new, having been opened in 1979 under the leadership of Rev. Leslie Jobb who was from Belmont. Les, like Rev. Gordon Delaney and Rev. John Beers, had known my uncle Rev. George Hadley when he ministered in the Debert district in the late 1950's. However, the new Avonport Church still did not have a steeple. Clara Daisy Duncan, a keen member of the church, decided to jumpstart the process of obtaining a steeple by starting a steeple fund. Clara's granddaughter Pauline is now a Baptist Minister and Chaplain herself. She officiated when Donna and I got married in June, 2012.

The folks wondered where they'd find someone to build a steeple, so in an (innocent or blatant) act of nepotism, I told them that Warren Manthorne of Seal Harbour had been building steeples for churches in Guysborough County. So, they arranged for Warren to construct the steeple.

While I was waiting for Warren to arrive from Seal Harbour, I drove down to Avonport Beach for a break and to see how the old cabin was looking for summer. As I was coming back along the Beach Road at the Railroad Crossing, I heard a screaming whistle. I suddenly realised that it was not a Johnny Cash song but the Dayliner that ran between Halifax and the Valley, warning me to get off the tracks. The Engineer, Gerry Parks, was so certain that he had hit me that he stopped the Dayliner and backed it up towards the crossing. He saw me standing safely by my car, my hands in the air in abject apology to him, and then he shook his fist at me and went on down the line. Whenever I see him at the Pereaux Church in the summers, I always greet him by singing, 'I Hear the Train A Coming'."

Rev. Pauline Coffin of the Avonport Church offered this heart-warming tribute to Gary:

"Gary Manthorne was the first minister that I ever met. He was serving in Avonport and Lockhartville Baptist churches and was my grandmother's pastor. He was her favourite and soon became like one of the family.

For a minister, he seemed pretty cool. But I began to discover Gary had a whole other side. The realisation began slowly. With his booming voice and huge beard, some of the children in Sunday School were convinced that he was not just the pastor but indeed God himself.

Years later, I began my own journey with Christ and subsequent call to ministry. It was then that I began to see how popular Gary was in the Valley. It seemed like everyone and their dog knew Gary. I thought at first that this popularity was only a Nova

Scotia phenomenon. However, while I was preaching in Vancouver, a lady came over to me to ask if I knew Gary Manthorne. I began to suspect that his popularly may be national.

His popularity spilled over to the feline population when he began a pastoral relationship with my cat, Ralph. True to his quirky sense of humour, Gary left a phone message for me on the answering machine. Instead of directing it to me, he left it for Ralph asking her to let me know that he had called. Every time I would play back the message Ralph would come running, totally convinced that Gary was her private pastor.

Over the years, Gary continued to be a part of the family and well-loved by my parents. He has walked alongside our family through some celebrations but also through many sad times. It was with joy that I was able to help him with a celebration last year. I officiated at his secret, backyard wedding to Donna last summer. Thanks Gary!"

The following was contributed by Lolita Crosby of the Avonport Church;

"When I was approached to see if I would be interested in submitting something for a book to be published about Gary, I was taken aback and my immediate thought was whether I could write anything of interest; on the other hand I felt honoured to be asked. So, in the next few paragraphs I will endeavour to put thoughts to words and try to do justice to our beloved Gary.

It was when I worked in Wolfville in the 1960's that I first heard the name Gary Manthorne. One evening in 1982 while attending a celebration for a relative of mine in the Melanson Hall, I met Gary.

I was on the pulpit committee for the Avonport United Baptist Church and I asked him if he would be interested in coming to Avonport. He indicated that I could put his name forward. I did and August 1, 1982, Gary began his ministry in the Avonport - Lockhartville United Baptist Pastorate. He remained with us until January 1988. His ministry with us and our love for him is best explained in the following words penned by the late Charlotte King and is printed below with permission from her daughter Sheila East. These words were sung by the choir to the tune "Fairest Lord Jesus" on Gary's last service with us.

Tribute to the Rev. Gary Manthorne
- by the late Charlotte King

How truly blessed were we, when our Pastor said that he
Would heed the call - Plainly we all could see
The answer to our need was here.
No stranger to hard work, duties he did not shirk.
When trouble came he was always there
To comfort and sustain, to help to ease the pain
Of those who needed one to care.
His sermons we enjoyed. Of humour they weren't void.
We didn't know what was coming next.
But underneath it all, we heard the gospel call.
The Bible was his earnest text.
It's hard to see him go, we're sure to miss him so.
His friendly nature is loved by all.
This is our fervent prayer. God keep you in his care,
While answering this - God's latest call.

During Gary's (Rusty) time with us, he along with my late husband Bill Crosby (Hawkeye), Prof. Marie McCarthy (Bubbles) and Faye Sponagle (Rainbow) started the first Beaver Troop in Avonport.

We consider Gary to be our own family pastor. He presided at the wedding of my brother and his wife. He was the minister when both my mother and father passed away. He was there for an uncle's funeral which necessitated traveling to Leamington for a committal service. Gary also attended funerals for two of my brothers and conducted the service for a brother-in-law. At my most difficult time, Gary was there to assist in the memorial service for my late husband and to provide his comforting words.

After his service as Pastor in our community he kept in touch with my family and when a carpenter was needed Gary agreed to be that carpenter. My husband always looked forward to Gary's visits when they would share a lunch of salt fish, potatoes and once in a while, bread and molasses. On these occasions, I usually left the men to be boys again. Gary's great memory for names has always amazed not only me but most everyone.

I have no appropriate words that would describe this man adequately but close simply with the thought that he exhibits the true spirit of God through his Christian example and his interaction with all."

Lolita also introduces the poem by Annie Bird.

"It was well known by most people that Gary liked country and western music. He could be found on just about every Friday night at the

Legion jam sessions and Gary was a favorite MC for a lot of the fundraising shows around the Valley. When someone was up against hard time from sickness or loss of work, Gary was often contacted to arrange such a show. At that time, the local bands and groups would rally round and donate their time and talent. Often the local businesses would donate goods and service. Gary's good-natured manner and spontaneous humour would always gather a crowd. The following, is a poem written from a compilation of country song titles and lines. It was sung to the tune of "Vaya Con Dios", as a tribute to Gary when he was moving on to another pastoral charge."

From Deep in the Waters of Love - by Annie Laurie Bird-Feb, 1988

We know he isn't perfect, but he didn't claim to be,
When he made a left and then a
right to this community.

Now he's got leavin' on his mind, he's "Gotta' Travel On".
Sure, a "Little-Bitty Tear" will fall
the minute "He's Gone".

His name became a household word; he never sings the blues.
Give the good ol' boy a country
send-off, listen to the clues.

"The Easy Part's Over Now"; his rowdy friends
shall not be moved.
"He's so Easy to Love"; he's no
falling star, that's been proved.

It's alright, He took those chains from our hearts,
now we're "Born Free".
We'll not take "One Step Forward and
Two Steps Back", just you see.

"Smile the While", for we know the Lord's been
mighty good to us.
Don't fall to pieces. Let's pretend all
our troubles soon will pass.

Now we are dancing "The Good-bye Waltz", and
walking the line too.
When we hear the sound of distant
drums we'll get over you.

Though his boots were made for walking, someday
he'll fly away.
Safe on the "Wings of a Dove", when
comes that "Unclouded Day".

Oh Lord, "It's Hard to be Humble", "Somewhere
Between Ragged and Right".
Who's gonna' fill his shoes on a
"Tennessee Saturday Night"?

We let the stars get in our eyes now we're "Looking
Back to See",

There goes our reason for living – "My
Old Brown Coat and Me".

Twinkle, twinkle, lucky star – with eyes of love we'll
sing, sing, sing.
Loving him came easy now isn't
that the strangest thing!

"Just for You" we'll still love someone we've known
a long, long time.
Your tender loving care will always
be gentle on our minds.

Don't send the pillow you dream on your last letter
bore the news.
With "Pins and Needles" in our hearts,
we'll be "Moanin' the Blues".

"Heaven's Just a Sin Away" – those hot biscuits
make him think.
A "Tragic Romance" with salt herring,
then "Cool Water" his drink.

Food's an old flame in his heart, with eyes of love
he dares to dream,
Of Sweet Temptation, like pie; apple,
cherry, mince and chocolate cream.

"Amanda" and "Peggy Sue", with "Jealous Heart"
were left behind,
Cause all the time it was, "Linda"
ever gentle on his mind.

Sharing His Great Love

"What's He Doing in My World?" "My Lips are
Sealed"! That's alright.
"If You Loved Me" half as much there'll
be "No Tear Drops Tonight".

If they were on some "Foggy Mountain Top" yearn-
ing for to spoon,
"For the Good Times", they'd head "Down
Yonder" 'neath the "Cajun Moon".

"Old Flames Can't Hold a Candle to You". "You
Light up My Life",
Then sail for "Bluebird Island" with "Your
Woman", your woman, your wife!

Though he never picked cotton, he's lived a lot in
his time,
And drove "In the Misty Moonlight"
with gas bought for a dime.

He's "On the Backside of 30", so 'Don't Fight the
Feeling" -
There's a Grand Old Opry Show
playing somewhere in Wheeling.

Down around the bend in the water to "The
Fishing Hole"
He sings the "Barefoot Boy Blues",
"Way Down Deep" in his soul.

Well he might have "Gone Fishin" leaving
"Footprints in the Sand",

But he loves those "Dear Hearts and
Gentle People", you understand.

This highway leads to heaven, "Jesus, Don't Give
Up on Me".
As he serves "The Church in the
Wildwood", "Oh What a Love" we see.

"Settin' the Woods on Fire", "Down in the Valley",
oh what bliss.
Just give him 40 acres. "Love Can't
Ever Get Better than this".

Like that "Old Time Religion", we wouldn't
change him if we could.
Though, he leaves us "Crying in the
Chapel", in a "Lonesome Mood".

He loved us everyone, big, little and short and tall.
Oh weary soul, the book of memo-
ries, he filled for us all.

Just a "Tumbleweed", "Blowing in the Wind", he
keeps wandering on,
"Summer, Winter, Spring and Fall", we
did it our way, "Now He's Gone".

When he heads up "Cripple Creek' listening to
Tanya Tucker,
You can bet your "Bottom Dollar" he'll
hear "Yonder Comes a Sucker".

There are "Diamonds in the Rough", just "Pictures from Life's Other Side".
'It's All in the Game", "Farther On",
"Whispering Hope" will abide.

If we "Keep on the Sunny Side", we will always learn, it's true.
He can melt our "Cold, Cold Heart"
and find "The Rainbow's End" too!

When we travel down the "Lost Highway", sing us "Back Home Again",
"It's a Sin" anytime to see "Blue
Eyes Crying in the Rain".

When the angels "Carry us Home", "One Minute Past Eternity",
If you're still within the sound of
my voice "Remember Me".

"Silver Threads and Golden Needles" – "Funny How Time Slips Away".
We'll never get out of this world
alive, so some folks say.

"It's Such a Pretty World", wildwood flowers grow in the dale.
"All His Children" don't want to see
the "Old Log Cabin for Sale".

"No-one Will Ever Know", "All of the Monkeys Aren't in the Zoo".

"Our Heart has a Mind of its Own". "May
the Good Lord Bless and Keep You".

May the sun always shine on your "Mansion on the
Hill",
And "May You Always" have a
"Bluebird on Your Windowsill".

There's a cloud in our valley of sunshine, "Just for
You".
"We Almost Had It All", then,
"The bird of Paradise" flew.

On that "Orange Blossom Special", the time comes
to depart.
As "The Yellow Rose of Texas", he
left his brand on our hearts.

Like a "Bridge over Troubled Waters", for us "He
Made a Way".
May the Lord build him a "Cabin
in Glory Land" "Someday".

"Happy Trails" to you until we meet again we're
going to love you
Forever and ever – "Forever and Ever, Amen".

CHAPTER EIGHT

The Circuit Ridin' Preacher at Bethany Memorial Church - Aldershot

March, 1988 to November, 1995

"I have been very blessed with so many loyal, supportive friends during my years in the Annapolis Valley. I have also enjoyed that support through the 'mountains and valleys' of life itself, so to speak. When I was invited by Bethany Memorial Church in Aldershot to be their minister, once again crowds showed up for the Induction Service. Somebody said to me afterward that it was the first time that they ever had to line up to get into church.

The congregation, having been through some stressful times, was ready to move ahead. We welcomed 90 new folks into membership during those years and Garnet Turner and the boys installed 5 new pews to handle the attendance. Danny Turner and his construction crew took up the contract to build the spacious Christian Education Centre. They did a lot of the interior work and then it was finished-up by the men of the church.

Another devoted brother combo was Don and John Rafuse, who between them were involved in every office and committee in the church, except the Ladies Auxiliary. John decided to join me in a trip to Seal Harbour one summer, having heard the occasional reference to this 'seaside resort'. He didn't seem to realise how far away it was. When we got to Truro, he asked if we were almost there. I had to say, 'err... ah... no John, not half-way yet'.

Then there was the time at the supper table (with my family) that I accidentally dropped my hearing aid. Haley the dog (always quick to catch a falling crumb) quickly grabbed it and chewed it up. Apparently, I must have said something about it at church because from then on John would often say that the dog could hear better than I could. Come to think of it, THAT was always true."

Here are some words from Donna Turner from Bethany Memorial Church in Aldershot:

"Gary presided over a funeral for my brother-in law in January 1991. It was a terribly stormy day with blizzard like conditions. My husband Dan offered Gary his four wheel drive truck to take home. We were worried about the road as the plough had not been through and visibility was poor at our house. He had a long drive to Gaspereau ahead of him. When Dan offered Gary the truck, he pondered the offer with a raised eyebrow and quickly inquired as to whether or not the radio would get C104: just an absolute comedian, as if to pretend he would risk the drive in his car had the radio selection not included C104.

Throughout the years Gary has always connected with the kids and has always made them feel important. He never forgets any details of the family and it was always a big thing to them when he visited. Our daughter Gail had her wisdom teeth out and Gary always just 'knew' these things. Or a little birdie would tell him. He showed up for a visit with a Dairy Queen milk shake and didn't leave without asking us and the kids if there were any special prayer needs. He had nick names for all of them and never forgot them. One summer during Vacation Bible School he made the mistake of letting our red-headed daughter trim his red beard. It became a common request after that.

Even now that all of our children are grown adults, they will find a way to bump into Gary or email him a heavy prayer request as they all feel so connected to him and cherish their relationship with him. He is so willing to listen and offer his unique wisdom and outlook, whether on a sad subject or a high life achievement.

This particular memory is so special. Some of my siblings don't have a close relationship with God and struggled as we all did when my father fell ill. Dad's minister, when he did visit, made it a point of mentioning or offering to collect his tithes. That always made everyone feel like Dad wasn't important to him and merely the visit was for financial support. From the beginning, Gary was always special to my Dad and it's no wonder – two comedians at play! We don't recall one single day that Gary didn't visit, during that eleven week span when Dad was in the hospital. If a nap or a nurse interfered, he would leave a note with his 'signature' – his trademark happy face hand-drawn complete with chin whiskers! What a comfort that logo offered us, a bright spot and a guaranteed laugh when we needed it most.

All of my siblings commented on Gary's dedication to visiting Dad and supporting our family during our darkest days. Gary of course, never expected anything in return and to this day is the closest connection they have to the Lord.

It was a unanimous vote that he was best suited last year to provide the service for our mom after her passing. Knowing that we all had the hardest time grieving our dad, largely because of the most impersonal funeral service, Gary tied our healing for both of our parents into an incredible service that served as a tribute to each of them, but also as the closure and acceptance that our entire family had yearned for. All of my kids and extended family commented on how comforting it was to sit in Mom's church and hear that familiar voice offer condolences, the comfort of the Lord's plan for Mom and our most treasured memories."

Gary has proven time and time again that no matter how sad the day might be, he is so capable of comforting all in his surroundings with God's word and his own humour! He is so humble and often naive of the absolute blessing he is. We're so thrilled for him and Donna and grateful to you Heather, for ensuring that this disciple of the Lord is being acknowledged for the incredible impact he has on his community, congregation, family and friends. We couldn't love him more!"

While Gary was at Aldershot his friend the late Rev. Alex Smith was going through a personal health challenge. Here are some words from Ellen Beaumont (Harold) formerly Ellen Smith

(Alex). "Here are some of my personal thoughts and remembrances of Rev. Gary over a period of about 30 years. Most of my contact with him took place over the five years when our family lived at the parsonage in Gaspereau. My late husband Alex and Gary were good friends. Gary often dropped by our home on either business or informal visits. I learned something of his character and personality traits, as we gradually got to know and love him.

True friendship is a treasured commodity and this one is firmly cemented, showing its strength on many occasions. Alex's years of illness were often filled with pain. Latterly, almost daily I drove him to the E.K.M. hospital to receive injections of Demerol to ease his suffering. Late one evening, on a holiday weekend, after he had been given his quota of pills and injections, he was again in pain and could not rest. At his wit's end he asked me to call Gary for any suggestions that might help him. I had exhausted, for his comfort, any supply of emergency resorts, we had at home.

Gary said, 'Just wait. I will see what I can do for you.' Within an hour I answered a knock at the door and there stood another faithful friend. He produced something that they thought might help. Sure enough, not much later, the patient finally relaxed and was able to get some sleep. To me, that sums up true friendship in a nutshell.

Now I turn to another side of Gary's nature; a warmth of love that really stood out. The last days of Alex's life were spent in the E.K.M (Eastern Kings Memorial) hospital in Wolfville. Every day with regularity, Gary paid a visit. They had many 'tete-a-tetes', sharing stories and personal experiences.

One day in September of 1988, Alex was given the dreaded news that he would not be alive to see Christmas. Gary came in shortly thereafter. This was the most emotional scene, seeing these two men sobbing in each other's arms. I watched in silence, keeping my feelings to myself. Following the initial shock, the two discussed funeral wishes and plans. I clearly remember Alex's remark, 'Gary, you are my best friend. I want you to conduct a good part of my service.' This was indeed what took place very soon after this discussion. For Gary it must have been particularly stressful as that very day was Gary's birthday. He did a masterful job and to this day has remained my fast friend.

When the major family business was completed, it was time to do all the more detailed, private tasks. One mammoth task was wondering what to do with Alex's considerably large library. I chose what books I thought the family should keep and piled the remainder on a desk top in the study. I was moving from the parsonage to a new home so I phoned Gary and gave him first choice of the books. Time went by, not days or weeks but into the next months. When next I saw Gary he told me the reason for not taking the books. My innermost feelings had been correct as Gary told me there was too much sentiment and emotion attached to his friendship with Alex. He felt that he could not bring himself to examine the books. From this I saw the more warm and loving side of this precious friend.

Both of our sons have their special memories of Gary as well. At present, James, the elder, is studying for the Christian ministry at Acadia University and is finding good use for his father's library. He keeps contact with Gary who is always interested in his progress.

Thirteen years ago I remarried to Rev. Harold Beaumont and we have kept a great relationship with Gary. We have had many humorous times together and when he comes to visit we always try to have a supply of his favourite beverage, chocolate milk."

Author's note: To this day, Gary carries a coffee mug with either coffee or chocolate milk when he is preaching. It is just part of his 'signature'.

CHAPTER NINE

The Circuit Ridin' Preacher in Clarence

November, 1996 to August, 2003
Wolfville Ridge - November, 1998 to September, 2004

Notes from Gary:

"During the time that I was suspended from the ministry, I picked up my old hammer and saw again and did some carpentry work for Dick Haliburton on his farm in Avonport. When my year was up, Area Minister Rev. John Beers put me in touch with the congregation at Clarence in Annapolis County. They were a devoted group of only 13 members which was quite a change from Aldershot's 150. Bruce Rand asked me a couple years into it how it was going in Clarence and I replied that it was going good and that I had started with 13 and still had 11. I never told him 'til years later that eventually it had perked up to 22. It was wonderful to be with the Clarence folks although I was still wrestling with inner distresses and didn't really give the congregation and community the degree of attention they deserved. Nonetheless, they too were very kind and it is still a delight to see any of them from time to time."

Author's note:

Although Gary may have felt that he was not giving his best in Clarence because of his own personal challenges, I got a different story from Joe Johnson. Joe confided to me that when Gary arrived there, Joe was having some marital difficulties. He had married a Jewish girl and had converted for their children. Things had deteriorated to the point where Joe was spending as many hours away from home as possible. One morning at about 4:00AM on a Sunday, while Joe was in the wood pile splitting wood, he felt 'lead' to go to church. Of course Gary, seeing a new face in church, showed up at Joe's house the very next day and their friendship began. Joe said that Gary still means the world to him and had helped him through a very difficult time in the past. Gary also baptised Joe.

Joe got his divorce and later married Natalie who was also divorced. Natalie attended the Clarence Church. In December of 2000, Gary performed their wedding ceremony. During the ceremony the best man and the bride's maid started to laugh. They were looking down at Gary's feet which sported a pair of 'Duckies' (heavy, rubber, boot-style shoe), although he was dressed in a suit. They still smile over that but they told me that Gary was right to wear them because later the temperature dropped and it became very snowy and slushy outside.

Joe told me that Gary always kept his attention in the services and he remembers one Sunday when Gary pulled from under the pulpit, the axe Gary's father always used to slaughter a hen for dinner at

Christmas and Thanksgiving . Gary had become quite attached to the hens and he saw them as his 'friends', so he always had mixed feelings about the wonderful chicken dinners at such otherwise happy times.

Joe also declared that he and Natalie would do anything in the world for Gary. I met Joe and Natalie when Joe played the guitar and they sang at a celebration of Gary's 41 years in the ministry at the Forest Hill Baptist Church.

Now back to Gary's story:

"The church at Clarence could not afford to pay a full-time salary, so it was a good fit for my life and schedule when the Wolfville Ridge Church, just a couple kilometers from home, invited me to team up with them as well. Both congregations adjusted the time of their Sunday morning service to make it work, allowing for the 50 minute commute between the two. During the Wolfville Ridge years, I became increasingly involved in various fund-raising projects. They were primarily variety shows for situations of need. At one point, one might have thought that we had all of the problems of the Valley under control because we put on a show to support the farmers out west. They were suffering a drought and therefore had a poor hay crop. I got my musical buddies together. Alton Allen, Charlton Levy and Curtis Rowe met me in Melanson for a photo shoot in Bill Anderson's barn. Our local paper, the Kentville Advertiser, used that picture to promote our 'Country Hay-Down' benefit show. We raised over $700.00 as a vote of support by the Eastern farms for the Western farms. To paraphrase the late Ralph Klein, we DIDN'T want those Western cows to starve in the drought.

Alton Allen, Charlton Levy, Curtis Rowe, Gary at Bill Anderson's barn.

I was making an effort in those years to get some exercise. Along with my dog Haley, I would walk uphill, downhill and all around the streets of Wolfville. One evening we stopped in at the Wolfville Legion and were immediately asked to leave. Although I was often at Legion events, I hadn't learned some of the protocol such as, 'take your hat off, and no dogs allowed'. So, we continued up the street. Near the Save Easy store we ran across Bill and Necia Meisner who were members of the Wolfville Ridge Church. I told them of this latest disgrace and Bill's not so empathetic reply was (in the Johnny Cash style of course), 'Don't take your dog to town son, leave your dog at home son, don't take your dog to town'.

However, I am a slow learner and Haley and I took a lot more walks in Wolfville. One Saturday evening we stopped (this time at the Lions' Hall) realising there was music playing inside that for once, didn't involve me. As I entered the hall, I let Haley free from her leash and she went strolling down the centre aisle enjoying people patting her. When the fellow on stage saw what was going on he interrupted his song and switched to the obvious old-time Elvis number, 'You Ain't Nothing but a Hound Dog'."

Best friends

CHAPTER TEN

The Circuit Ridin' Preacher in Seal Harbour

2004 – 2008

Author's Note:

I recently spoke with Keith Luddington and his wife Bessie from Seal Harbour. Keith told me that Gary has been a very close friend to them. In the last two years of his first wife Shirley's life, Gary was a regular visitor and they were most impressed with his powerful prayers. Shirley always felt much better when Gary visited.

Keith says, "On December 28, 2007, I took a heart attack and was hospitalised an hour and a half away from home. The doctor told me that I needed to go to Halifax but there was no room and he would not be able to get me in until after the New Year. He would give me a nitro drip but that was all they could do.

My son had brought Shirley to visit in her wheel chair and just after they left, Gary came in. I explained the situation to Gary and he said, 'I would like to pray'. He talked to God as if God were sitting right there between us. He asked God to make a way for me to go to Halifax, and to save my life so that I could look after Shirley. After Gary left, a nurse came in at 3:00PM and said, 'I have 20 minutes to get you ready for Halifax.' Not even the doctor could believe it was happening."

Gary had the funeral for both Keith's wife and Bessie's husband. Sometime after that, Keith and Bessie wanted to get married. They remembered that before Gary left Seal Harbour to go back to the Valley, Les Livingston (a well- known singer in the Valley) and Charlotte Brydon (his fiancé) had eloped from the Valley to Seal Harbour to be married by Gary. Ward and Ivy Sangster were asked by Gary to be their witnesses. Keith thought that it would work well in reverse for them, so they came from Seal Harbour to the Valley and were married in Gary's back yard. Gary asked life-time Valley residents Charlton and Marie Levy, a couple they had never met before, to stand for them.

Gary comments on those years:

"During those recent four years back in the churches of my childhood, Vernon Zwicker and I would often enjoy a good meal at Audrey Cooke's. Audrey was Organist at both Goldboro and Isaac's Harbour. As well, she was both the church clerk 'and' the treasurer at Isaac's Harbour. Sherm and Leona McArthur's devotion and loyalty to the Goldboro Church has kept it open and it stands as a lovely edifice along the Atlantic Shore. In New Harbour, I enjoyed wonderful times around Ward and Ivy Sangster's table, after which we would retire to their living room to analyse the mysteries of life.

Lorne and Wanda Jamieson and Lloyd and Hazel Nickerson were people who would frequently invite a house full of us, for special occasions. Vonnie Jack's devotion to the church as Clerk and Treasurer keeps the lights on and the doors open at Seal Harbour Church. Each year till I moved back to the Valley, Vonnie hosted a Christmas party for me at her house to bring together the people of the four churches.

And how's this for a wonderful coincidence? My school 'bus' (panel truck) driver of 1959-60, was my next-door neighbour when I lived there in the New Harbour Parsonage. What a neighbour he was! He ploughed my driveway in the winter and helped me saw up my wood in the summer.

Here's yet another wonderful coincidence of life. When I was still a kid at home, Mary and Angus Luddington would often visit Mom and Dad on a Sunday evening after Church. As they talked on, I'd go to bed and read among other things, a chapter from my New Testament. Forty- five years later, Mary too is a Parsonage neighbour and Secretary of the Parsonage Committee. She was always asking me what could be done to make my home more comfortable. I thought they had done a great job of installing the wood furnace in my first winter back and making the old, drafty house a snug place to live. She combined the qualities of Jesus' friends Mary and Martha in showing such genuine love and support while attending to the practical duties of home and table.

My most regular munch and lunch stop was at Everett and Muriel Fanning's in Seal Harbour. When it came close to meal time Everett would look at his watch and say to Muriel either, 'It's five minutes to, here he is' or on alternate days, 'I guess Gary's not coming today.' I would have assumed that he was relieved on the days I didn't show up but Muriel still tells me how much they both enjoyed the three of us getting together every couple of days around their table. It would often end up afterwards with me 'napping it off' on their living room couch.

That reminds me of Lew and Evelyn Gammon's kids telling me that when I used to have dinner with their folks in Pereaux thirty years ago, I'd sometimes grab a nap on their kitchen couch afterwards. No wonder that counsellor told me I wasn't suitable for the ministry and should learn to operate a backhoe. A backhoe fellow would carry a lunch can and have better manners."

CHAPTER ELEVEN

2009-2013 Four Years of Many Changes

Upper Vaughn

"I'll always be grateful to the good folks of Upper Vaughan for being the answer to my prayers as to whether I would have another Valley ministry before retirement. However, it turned out to be a brief ministry because I couldn't resist and didn't try to resist, the invitation to go back after thirty years to Pereaux. I was to share the ministry there with Mark Parent. Like me, Mark had previously been a minister there. As many people know, Mark grew up in Bolivia while his parents were serving as missionaries there. The closest I ever came to being a missionary was in 1978, when I told Mom I was going to the Pereaux Church and she thought I was going to the South America Country of Peru, as a missionary.

This second round in Pereaux was meant to be an interim situation but it actually continued for 3 years, until March, 2013. In the meantime, the Forest Hill Church at the top of Gaspereau Mountain had invited me to minister with them, which I was able to co-ordinate while also being at Upper Vaughan. I continued with Forest Hill while at Pereaux and I am still there now.

I had known the Forest Hill folks from 40 years earlier when I was just a couple of kilometers down the hill in the Gaspereau Valley churches. The Forest Hill Church has a caring congregation (as all churches surely should have) where members watch out, not only for each other's needs, but for the people in the community around the church. I feel blessed to be with them in my semi-retirement state."

Author's note:

To have Gary as a pastor at Forest Hill Church is a unique experience. We have a brunch on the second Saturday of every month where Gary can be seen catching up in conversation with someone from his past or meeting a new friend. At our annual July fun day we can count on Gary to be there for the whole event. The following picture shows Marion Gertridge, one of the Deacons of the church, who appears to be admiring Gary's new green-blue sneakers at our yard sale.

Gary and Marion Gertridge

Of course the gospel music goes on all afternoon, highlighting just about every local group we can think of. Gary always stays until the very last song.

Also, we host a variety show a couple of times a year where Gary is our Master of Ceremonies. Our services are held on Sunday afternoon at 2:30PM and when Gary is away the church family generously allows me to do the service, along with my music duty of playing the organ. We are truly the friendly, 'little white church' on the side of the road.

Forest Hill Baptist Church

The author's granddaughter Allyson Thomas
raised money for the Forest Hill Church.
Here, she is recognised by Gary at the
30th Seal Harbour Reunion in 2013

Here are some words from Rev. Dr. Mark Parent, Gary's Co-Minister in Pereaux:

"How does one sum up Gary Manthorne and his work as an ordained minister? In many ways, I think it is by looking back at some of the great Kings County ministers of the past who did not confine themselves to the walls of the organised church but who saw their ministry as one which extended beyond the institutional church to all people. As the church has become a more marginal institution within society, such greats of the past have disappeared and ministers have confined themselves within the walls of the church and tailored their outreach accordingly.

Gary does not do that. He values the institution of the church but sees the call to ministry in much broader and far less institutional terms than most of his contemporaries. This matches his theological understanding of the Christian faith which is simple in its articulation and built upon the affirmation that God is a God of love who cares for us in the midst of the trials and tribulations of this life, with all our warts and failings. While he relates equally to all, his lack of pretence makes him especially popular with those whose financial well-being or community stature is not high. He is very much a 'man of the people'.

In the institutional setting of the church, this means that Gary is less interested in programs and more interested in people. His preaching style is conversational and his message always comes around to the theme of God's love and the call to share that love with others.

A Seal Harbour boy, Gary values his community roots and often talks about his childhood growing up in rural Nova Scotia. In fact, one Sunday, I joked that Gary must think that for Seal Harbour residents a phone call to God is a 'local' not a long distance call. It is these rural roots which have shaped his ministry style - reaching out to the whole community, not just church goers, and of treating everyone the same - be they wealthy or poor.

Gary also has a keen sense of humour and likes to poke fun at himself. He usually tries to leave a visit or a church service with a smile on people's faces. In part, I think that this is due to the fact that Gary had struggles at school growing up due to congenital hearing problems and so values laughter and happiness and tries to impart it to others. I joked once that Gary and I had a good relationship; one that was pure and simple - I was pure and he was simple. Sure enough he found an appropriate comeback and the laughter I elicited by my comment was built upon by his self- depreciating reply.

Finally, Gary is known for his appetite and his unerring ability to land in on parishioner's homes right at meal time. Indeed, one member of the church told me they woke up one morning to find him cooking breakfast in their kitchen!

Since 2010, Gary and I have been working in a co-ministry team at the Pereaux Baptist Church. His steady, unflappable style and his unerring love for the people of the community have been an inspiration. He will go down as one of Kings County's greatest ministers, not because he preached in big and wealthy churches but because he treated the community at large as a church and has been treated by the community at large as their pastor even when they have failed to 'darken the door of a church'. Gary has taken the church and, more importantly, God's love to them."

CHAPTER TWELVE

Roasting Gary - Some Funny Stories Lovingly Told

The Case of the Missing Hamburger - Mrs. Ellen Beaumont

"While my first husband Rev. Alex Smith was still living, Gary often visited us. We soon found out that Gary really enjoyed the consumption of food and his sense of humour was, and still is, tremendous. I remember clearly one particular day when Gary came to visit. The boys had eaten lunch and were in the living room watching TV. We were visiting with Gary in the kitchen probably enjoying a cup of tea. Later, after Gary had departed, James came to me and said, 'Mom, I'm hungry. Where is my other hamburger? I left it on the plate.' Well, though I had not witnessed the disappearing act, it was not difficult to discern who the culprit was. Gary remembers this incident, as we have had many good laughs over it."

Gary's Singing - Told to the Author by Gary

Everyone knows how much Gary likes to sing. With his hearing problem apparently he used to sing a little too loudly and his mother, who was also his school teacher, told him just to mouth the words in the Christmas concert. However, that did not put a damper on Gary's serenading later in life.

More Singing

This incidence is reported by Gary's good friend Alex Smith:

"On May 30th, 1975, I was awakened at 5:00AM by someone singing under my bedroom window. It was Gary's way of announcing the birth of his first born son, Allan."

Another Singing Story - the Author

One of Gary's favourite pieces at Christmas time was O' Holy Night. Gary emails me every week to give me the hymns for the Sunday Service, usually commenting on how fast the week had rolled around once more. One of my favourite solos also is "O' Holy Night" and I was thrilled when Gary asked me to sing it on Christmas Eve. I remember thinking that the piece was one of Gary's favourites and I knew that he would rather be singing it himself. It seems I was correct because before the time arrived, Gary got back to me with a very humble request to join me in the solo. So, for that Christmas Eve the solo became a single part duet and a good time was had by all.

A Funny Email

Here is an example of an email sent to me by Gary after a very rainy Saturday. It made me smile. If your spelling is bad, you will not catch the humour in this.

To me: After the Reign....We had brunch today. Usually brunch is on Saturday. Ergo, today is Saturday. Ergo Bergo - tomorrow is Sunday already. In witch kase - hims...430 - Showers of Blessing, 193 - God is so Good, 750 - Peace like a River.........

The Beard Wig - the Author

At one point in his life Gary sported a long beard. His friend Marshall Jones from the Aldershot Church has very little hair. Marshall told me that one-time, Gary came up behind him and laughingly placed the beard on top of Marshall's head, giving the others around a chance to see their friend Marshall with hair.

- Gary, Believe it or not!

Free Trim, No Shave - Gary

"Clarence and Laura McCharles were among my Ridge families. One day I was visiting Clarence in his barn. While he was cleaning up around one horse, I was scratching the head of another horse. She responded to me by reaching out and chewing on my long beard. A few years later when Clarence was in his final days of terminal illness, I crawled up beside him on the bed and we talked about the things of life and death. At one point I said to him, 'Clarence, you know there is something I've been wondering about. Remember that day in the barn? Do you figure I owe you for a haircut or do you owe me for hay?' Clarence replied that he thought they should call it even."

Gary Offers this Humourous Anecdote: Are You Hungry?

"A bunch of us were sitting around the supper table at Glen Manthorne's old Seal Harbour homestead in the summer 2012, enjoying one of Theresa's sumptuous feasts. She asked me if I cooked a lot. I told her that for the 6 years that I had been living alone, I didn't even know if the oven worked in my kitchen stove. In seemingly intensive concern Theresa asked, 'You mean there were days when you went without anything to eat?' The others at the table 'laughed their heads off', knowing the truth about my irresponsible life-style of showing up at certain homes at meal times unannounced.

Looking for Business – the Author

Because of all of the funerals Gary does, I think over 1200 so far, he often gets lovingly teased about his so called, 'looking for business'. When my husband Lloyd, who is sometimes guilty of this teasing, was hospitalised for observation, he told me that Gary had come by for a visit. I thought that was good of him since he was not our pastor at the time, and I enquired about their conversation. Lloyd told me that the first thing Gary said was, "Lloyd, I am 'sorry' to see you looking so well". We both had a good laugh over that.

Political Fun

Just as Gary had his favourite Hockey team it was general knowledge that he preferred a particular political party as well. Ellen Beaumont tells this story:

"Somewhere around the Early 1980's, Rev. Alex and another student minister, also one of Gary's friends, decided to play a trick on Rev. Gary. It was election time and I don't recall if it was Federal or Provincial. Under cover of darkness they carried out their scheme. Having knowledge of political biased opinions of Gary and another well-known Valley man, they were aware that they were in total opposition with their views. Silently the co-conspirators drove to both homes, uprooted the election signs and switched them. Then they returned to their prospective homes. I have no knowledge of the owners' reactions when the ruse was discovered but I expect it was taken in good sport by both. Gary never knew who both guilty parties until our recent conversation revealed the names."

Also from Ellen Beaumont: A Postage Story

"I recently came upon a letter from Gary in answer to one that I had written to him. In his amusing way he thanked me, but wondered why a 'penny pinching' Scot would bother spending 50 or more cents on a stamp for such a character as he. I loved his sense of humour and I hope he will always keep it."

A story Gary told the Author: Pride before Fall

Upon bumping into a long- time friend, the subject of the friend's aging parents came up. His friend suggested that Gary drop in to see them sometime and told him they would be thrilled to see him. One day when the opportunity presented itself, Gary decided to call on the couple who did indeed seem overjoyed to see him. They told him how much they missed him and how they thought he was just such a wonderful person. Just as Gary was deeply basking in all of that glory over a cup of tea, one of them said, "We have missed you so much since you retired. We have never been able to find another *doctor* to replace you." Can't you just hear the air going out of that balloon? Gary never told them of their mistaken identification, but said his goodbyes and left.

Another Postage Story - the Author

Recently, I was involved in "The Coldest Night of the Year" walk for the homeless. Gary informed me that he would have a donation for me on Sunday. Since that would be after the walk and I wanted to get my funds in, I went online and paid the donation. True to his word Gary handed me an envelope on Sunday which I put in the bag with my music books. At home I retrieved from my music bag, a hand-made envelope which anyone would make in a pinch, but I had a great laugh when I noticed he had hand-drawn a stamp in the corner for 78 and 1/4 cents along with a hand-drawn smiley face. Gary always makes time to do things to make people smile.

A Memory Slip - the Author

In Church one Sunday, Gary told of an incident that happened on a student pastorate in New Brunswick. He was closing a prayer with "The Lord's Prayer" when suddenly his mind went blank in the middle of a prayer he had recited all of his life. For years after that he always had a copy of the prayer in front of him and only recently did he trust himself to repeat it by memory.

The Joke Was on Me - From Laurie Levy of White Rock

"One particular time Gary and Linda invited us for supper. My mother was 'keeping company' with Clyde Forsythe at the time and they came in shortly after we were finished eating. We thought it was strange for them to come as they knew we had been invited; however, we found out that they had been invited also. During the evening we joked around about Mom and Clyde getting married. Gary said, 'We could do it tonight. We have a preacher, a best man and a bride's maid.' We all laughed. I thought they would get married sometime but I didn't know when. Gary said, 'I think we should have a rehearsal, so when the time comes we will be ready and know what is going to take place.' We all agreed, only to find out that Gary had collaborated with Mom and Clyde and they were getting married right then. So, the joke was on us."

Also from Laurie - That Beard Again

"Everyone thought a lot of Gary and enjoyed his impromptu dropping in. One morning shortly after he came to Gaspereau, he dropped in and was offered a cup of tea. He said, 'Don't mind if I do' and promptly got up and served himself. That really broke the ice and our friendship evolved from there. Another time Gary endeared himself to us when he came by as we were having breakfast with our company, an uncle of mine from the United States. As there were no extra vehicles in the driveway, Gary didn't know we had company when he accepted our invitation to join us. I introduced him to our guests as our Pastor. Gary has always had a beard. During our breakfast my outspoken uncle commented that preachers should not have beards. It was an awkward moment for us but Gary took it in stride with no offence taken and we continued our visit."

Walk Softly and Carry a Big Lunch - the Author

One summer, Gary worked on the pulp boats that came into Country Harbour to collect up the wood that the woodsmen had been cutting for months. Some years later, in a visit back home to Seal Harbour, he stopped in (as always) to H. D. Manthorne's General Store, where as usual a bunch of the fellows were collaborating on life. Arth Salsman, who actually lived near the wharf where the boat docked, was with them this time. Gary said, "Hi, Arth. I'm Gary Manthorne. Remember me? I worked with you on the pulp boat back in 1963." Arth replied, "I don't remember you doing much work. All I remember is that big lunch can you carried." So you see, Gary's reputation for eating well, follows him far and wide.

Joe Johnson from Clarence told me this story - Disappearing Act

One afternoon Gary came to call when Joe was cooking ribs on the barbeque. Joe knew he didn't have enough ribs for everyone so he closed the barbeque and turned it off. He invited Gary in for a cup of tea and he said that Gary cleaned out the cookie jar. He finally told Gary that he had to go to work, so Gary left. Joe then went to the barbeque to finish cooking the ribs but all that was left on the grill was 7 charred bones. The fat had dripped on the coals and they continued cooking until there was no meat left. So Joe, I am thinking there is a lesson here somewhere. Had you shared the ribs at least you would have had a taste. This way, not only did you not have ribs, you had an empty cookie jar.

Baptism by Muck? - the Author

The folks at Avonport - Lockhartville are very familiar with this story:

Gary had a lot of baptisms while he was there. One particular group comprised of Merle Mailman, Sherry Mailman, Vernon Ruggles and Fos Fuller, decided they wanted an outdoor baptism in the Minas Basin, the site of the world's highest and lowest tides. Gary told them all that having grown up in Seal Harbour on the Atlantic ocean, he could obviously figure out which tide level would be best for the baptism. However, when they got to Penny Beach on Sunday afternoon, the tide was so low that they had to walk 'halfway to Parrsboro' through the muck, to reach enough water to baptise them. The folks on the shore could hardly see them in the distance.

Camp Fire Season - Bethany Keddy

"Gary never does anything half-heartedly. For example, Gary's idea of having a campfire is to build a camp, burn it down and have the fire department put out the fire."

I'm 'Gonna' Love You Forever - the Author

Paul Davison, a long-time friend of Gary's and a friend of mine, told me that he once told Gary that they would be friends 'til the end. When Gary asked if he could borrow ten dollars, Paul told him, "This is the end". When Gary and Paul are together the one-liners fill the air with rapid succession, but I have come to realise that it has to be spontaneous and to have someone try to repeat it later just does not work.

Of Cats and Dogs - the Author

Gary has a wonderful way with small children. Even they can appreciate his humour. Once when we were gathered in our back garden for the wedding of my daughter Kathleen, Gary decided to put my 3-year-old granddaughter Allyson at ease by reminding her that he had visited at her house. He asked her how her dog was doing and she answered him that she did not have a dog but she had a cat. Gary made her laugh when he said, "What, you mean to tell me that dog is a cat?"

Here is another example of Gary's addictive humour in an email.

On the Offensive - by Gary

TO: Nova Scotia Supreme Kort:

While the MLA expense cases make it through the Korts, I thought in the interests of transparency, I'd re-send you my financial statements of 1958.

Gary

Gary's expense and disbursement statement

Are You Serious? - the Author

When Joan Nowlan heard that when I first met Gary I didn't know quite what to think of him, she declared, "You are not the only one". Her first encounter with Gary was at a small church in Grand Pre, when she asked Gary to meet her there to arrange for him to do a Church Service. While she was waiting for Gary she noticed a man in a long beard standing nearby. She was wondering to herself what he was doing there. Joan approached the man and said, "Can I help you?". He said, "I am Gary Manthorne, the minister." In her surprise and out of character for Joan, it slipped out - "You're kidding!"

CHAPTER THIRTEEN

Gary's Darker Hours

Perhaps the reason that Gary relates so well to every-day people is because he has endured some of the same heartaches in his own life. He has 'walked a mile' in everyone's shoes without even being conscious of it.

Athanasius, the early church father said, "I can do nothing without the help of God, and that from moment to moment; for when, so long as we are on the earth, is there a single instant in which we can say we are safe from temptation or secure from sin?" Gary understands this quote perfectly and is aware of the traps we either avoid each day or that we silently slip into, and before we know it we have been judged by others on what they think are the facts.

During his ministry Gary found himself unemployed (for a short period of time) from the traditional church ministry; once when he was minister in Gaspereau, and for one year after he left Aldershot. I have heard him speak of the low experiences he has had and I know that he is grateful that God brought him through, when it seemed that he would not withstand the hurt, the depression and mental agony. We all have periods of questioning ourselves and our abilities. Many of us have also paused to wonder if we made the right choices or if we had the proper skill-set to complete the race we started. I guess the doubts creep in when we start thinking about how we could have possibly made it this far, with all of the baggage we carried. It should not surprise us then, that after Gary (having been beaten down by challenges in his youth), slugging it out for seven years at Acadia and years in the ministry, needed a period of refreshing. It seems to me that God may have prepared him for such a time by giving him the carpentry skills that allowed him to work - throughout this difficult time. Sometimes, physical labour can help to heal our spirits and our minds. In any case, it gave Gary the means to support his family and to build a family home.

One low spot was in 1977 when Gary decided to take a break. At that time, he was working in the Gaspereau Valley churches. Although all of the people were supportive, Gary's high expectations of himself caused him to feel inadequate in his ministry. During that year when he built his house, he consulted a counselor to discuss his ambiguities and seek clarification for the future. That counselor, previously unknown to Gary, concluded in one session that he wouldn't need to see Gary again. He said (as Gary previously mentioned) that Gary was unsuited for the ministry and should instead operate a backhoe.

Fortunately for all of us, the Pereaux Church contacted Gary about supply preaching for a couple of Sundays and then asked him to come as their regular minister. Gary says, "By this time I had come to terms with what I did and did not have to offer for ministry and realised that the churches I had already served had been fine with what I had to offer. Pereaux was a wonderful, warm and supportive place to start again."

Gary describes another such low spot that ended his ministry at Bethany Memorial Baptist, Church in November 1995:

"It all came crashing down for me – when I was disciplined by the Convention due to a complaint against me; a complaint that was later withdrawn. I was off-duty for a year and went through a heavy-duty time of counselling and reflective, meditative prayer with Dr. Cherry and Dr. Dennis Veinotte. It was a dark and depressing time in my life but I delved into some of the hurts and heartaches of my life and in the process came to understand myself better and moved on from old wounds that were soon healed.

Through it all, it was precious to have so much support from the people of the churches and communities, including Bethany Memorial Church. It was hurtful to know that there were some here and there who 'got a kick' out of me having a hard time, but it caused me to ask myself if I had sometimes rejoiced when other people were 'brought low'."

It was during one of these 'valley' experiences in Gary's life that my husband Lloyd and I first met him. I remember so well because it was a particularly good year for us financially and we decided to share the blessings. I sensed that Gary was having a struggle and decided that I would put together a Christmas package for Gary. The box included a certificate for a turkey, an assortment of homemade baked goods, cranberry sauce, candy and anything else I could think of to make things easier for him at Christmas time. We were living in Truro then and Lloyd pre-arranged a meeting with Gary at Tim Horton's and drove to the Valley to deliver the box.

The reason I am relating this story is because I asked Gary about this a while ago and he had no recollection of the event. Being the great record keeper that he is, he recently found in his appointment book where, in November of that year, he had an appointment with Lloyd. This spoke volumes to me about Gary's state of mind at that time. Gary says that it was not clinical depression but just, as some would say, a period of self-reflection. It was also the time of the long straggly beard and the cowboy hat that seemed to be his signature at the time.

Around that same time I wondered if Gary might need some way of working in the ministry and I mentioned to him that for a long time I had wanted to start a church for 'sinners only' and I was hoping I could find a pastor who would understand what I meant by that. Gary looked at me and in all seriousness said, "I would be a good pastor for that church because I am the biggest sinner there is." Things did not come together at that time but who would have known that (15 years later) Gary and I would be working together in the Forest Hill Baptist Church on Gaspereau Mountain, and collaborating on this book.

Here are some words of reflection from Rev. Harold Beaumont who remembers this time in Gary's life.

"One day while passing through town, I happened to meet up with Gary and I enquired how things were going. He replied, 'Not too badly, but slower than usual.' Upon further conversation, I found out that Gary had not had a church for quite some time. He told me that he was not employed at all at that time.

I approached Ken Roscoe, the owner of a construction company building PMQs at the base in Greenwood. They needed good carpenters. I recommended Gary and told Ken that Gary had built his own beautiful home for his family. Upon my recommendation, Ken told me to have Gary bring his tools and come to the site on Monday. When I next saw Ken I enquired about Gary's progress and was told, 'He is very good. We can use him full-time, and we are glad to have him.' Talent will always show itself. I always say it is an insult to call a chef a cook, or a cabinet maker a carpenter. It is a great honour for me to call Gary a long-time friend."

Along with his professional challenges, Gary also had some personal struggles.

Here are Gary's words on the subject.

"By the summer of 2004, Linda and I finally divorced after a long period of separation and I remarried. It seemed a nice way to start a new marriage to have the honor of being invited back home to Guysborough County to minister in the churches of my youth, including Seal Harbour. However, within several months we realised the marriage was a mistake, though after our separation we kept trying to start things up again from time to time. It was devastating to face the fact that my high principles of marriage for a life-time were in tatters, all the more so now with the second divorce. In addition, I was still (in my own mind) wearing the badge of being professionally disciplined and concluded I had probably worn out my ministerial welcome in the Valley by this time. I thought that I would probably retire from the ministry while still working in Guysborough County and then go back to the Valley.

I found that in my prayer life I was saying, 'Lord, if I am to have a Valley Church again before retiring, either YOU will have to tell somebody or they'll have to think of me on their own. I won't be looking for anything.' In the meantime, I was thinking of where I'd like to live in retirement.

Would I build on my other lot in Melanson or would I hope to find a nice little bungalow somewhere in the area? On my next trip to the Valley, I was driving in Melanson and realised that Sharon Walsh had a For Sale sign on her house. I went right in, practically bought it on the spot, and then had to be concerned about whether I would be able to rent it safely to someone in the months or years ahead 'til I retired to it. Within a month, Marvin Rafuse called from the Upper Vaughan Church in nearby Hants County and asked me if I'd like to talk to them about coming to their church. Talk about things working out! With another Valley Church that I didn't look for, I would be living in the house myself. So, the renting problem was solved.

Although the marriage failed and it was a desolate time to be so far away from my children, grandchildren and all of my Valley friends, the time back home in Guysborough County played a key role in my present and future well-being. To re-assure myself that I was as healthy as I thought I was, I took part in a Well Man's Clinic at the tiny 8 room Hospital in Guysborough Town. Much to my shock, the Clinic discovered that I had prostate cancer which was about to burst forth and spread, with all of the chaos that usually presents. I had never heard of a Well Man's Clinic anywhere else, and my PSA count had always read safe and low, so if I had not been living in Guysborough County at that exact time, my cancer by now (five years later) would at the least have made my life miserable and perhaps taken it altogether.

So, I am forever grateful that the dear folks of my childhood churches took me back home to Seal Harbour for that crucial time in my life, thereby contributing to my health and well-being. No wonder I identify so strongly with the words of the Apostle Paul in Romans 8:28, when he was in prison for being too excited about Jesus. 'And we know that all things work together for good for those who love God, who are called according to his purpose'."

Ah, Home

This seems an appropriate spot to include the words of Linda Manthorne, Gary's ex-wife, friend and mother of his two boys. "What I really want to add, as an 'insider', is that Gary is just as good and kind as he seems from the outside (sort of like Rita MacNeill). He was (and likely still is) the best husband anyone could ask for and the most concerned, caring, and loving father... and son, too. He was thoughtful and helpful always to his mom and dad. He was NEVER a complainer and always set out in a positive way to do any task. When he received church calls at home - (any calls actually), he always treated everyone with respect and caring and NEVER EVER rolled his eyes, or got off the phone and made any negative comment. He put others' needs ahead of his own, but looked after himself too.

We were together for 35 years and I couldn't have asked for a nicer, kinder, more helpful or generous partner. We still have a very positive regard for each other, and a good relationship. I am a very, very, lucky woman."

Author's Notes:

In 2012, having renewed their friendship two years before, Gary married Donna Spark (Biggs).

Donna is a lovely, soft spoken lady who absolutely completes Gary. I believe that the promise of God to Israel, in Joel 2:25 "I will restore to you the years the… locusts consumed…' is now coming true for Gary. Recently, Gary said that he went out into his back yard one night, looked up at the stars and thanked God for his life. We truly serve a God who renews and restores.

Gary and Donna

CHAPTER FOURTEEN

My Interview with Gary

Many of the stories about Gary lose some of their flavour if they are not told in his own words So, here I have decided to prompt Gary and let him elaborate in his own way.

Gary, would you tell us a little more about your life-long friend, Alden?

Alden's mother was one of my teachers, so he spent some of his childhood in Seal Harbour with me. Plus we're second cousins. When he got married, he and his wife bought an old house in Seal Harbour and they raised their family in the community. He just recently moved to the senior's apartments in Sherbrooke. Seal Harbour folks know him as the kindest neighbour anyone could ever have. He worked in the local mink ranches back when they were viable in our area and then worked in the Bickerton fish plant until recent retirement. He and I have been the best of friends our whole life to this day. He tells a dramatic story of the cabin fire aftermath.

Sadly since the time of this interview Alden has passed away.

Gary, Seal Harbour, where you came from, is an even more remote area than Sheet Harbour where I grew up. Was it difficult to find work so that you could earn your university tuition?

Well, the various Manthorne boys had developed the custom of going 'hand lining' with the regular fisherman in the summer. Since Dad worked at the fish plant and Neil Manthorne didn't have kids, I went fishing with Neil as Charles had done a few summers earlier. Hanging out at the cove in the boats, fish sheds and fish plants was our life as kids when school was out. One summer I managed, with Neil's assistance, to haul aboard a 62 pound halibut and got the high price of 20 cents a pound. Codfish sold for 3 cents a pound, the occasional haddock for 5 cents a pound and Pollock (I think) was 2 cents a pound.

The following summer, as we kids and the fishermen gathered at the shore of the cove while deciding if it was 'fit' to take the boats out, Brent Manthorne asked me if I was going to catch a halibut this summer. For a joke I said, 'Oh yes, I'll catch him today and he'll be bigger than last summer'. Nobody was more shocked than I was when exactly that happened - 105 pounds, a good boost in my savings for getting to Acadia in September. I asked Arch Manthorne recently if he remembered way back then, about me catching a halibut. He replied that indeed he remembered and that the regular fishermen were rather annoyed that a kid was catching halibut and they weren't; halibut was not an everyday catch at that point. I actually made as much from my 105 pound halibut as I made in total from the rest of my fish that summer.

Sharing His Great Love

It became obvious in the summers of 1963 and 1964 that I needed to scrape up some money any legitimate way I could, so, I split a truck load of wood for Aunt Amy and Aunt Stella. My bill came to $23 but they gave me $40 and said keep the change; their way of supporting my Acadia hopes. I also worked in Uncle Os' mink ranch and tore down Bryce Turner's barn in Goldboro, one board at a time.

I even went to Halifax when Charles got me a job for a couple of weeks where he'd started out – in the car wash on Lower Water Street. I earned nearly $5 a day on some days. While ministering in Avonport – Lockhartville in the 1980's, I referred to the car-wash job as a high, executive position with Irving – specializing in washing the right front fender. There were about ten of us working on each car as they were pulled along the line.

Another source of wealth for getting to Acadia was that when my parents started receiving the baby bonus for me in 1945 (an incentive from the Canadian government) they deposited into my own account at the Seal Harbour Credit Union, instead of using it for their own expenses. By the time I got to Acadia it had added up to just about the right amount to pay the tuition side of my Acadia bill.

Gary, being so far from home you would have had some miscellaneous expenses. How did you cope with those?

Along with my studies, I worked in the university dining hall and also Dr. Cherry (always to my rescue) managed to keep scraping up working bursaries, such as lugging mail bags to the Girls'

Residence and working in security – monitoring the premises. Oh, and I got the Edward Manning Saunder's Bursary of $200.

What was that for Gary?
(Somberly) Just for being needy.

Tell me more about the New Brunswick car fiasco.
Well I recall that a fellow graduate student gave me my first car just before I headed off to my first student pastorate near St. Stephen, New Brunswick in 1965. It was a 1955 Ford Consul which required a quart of oil every 50 miles or so. It was getting noisy one day, so I spent $24 at a garage getting the problem 'fixed', and a few minutes later as I was driving along, there was an awful BANG under the hood. I stopped and lifted the hood and there was a hole in the side of the block and a flaming fire in the oil pan. Being broke and with no car, I expected to have to go back to Seal Harbour for the summer. However, a car dealer heard of my plight and gave me a 1955 Austin (valued at $300) to support my ministry.

One afternoon, 12 of the kids from my Youth Group piled into the car and we drove a few miles to the Oak Bay sand beach for a swim. On the way, a policeman 'hauled us over' and when he counted up the crowd in the car he observed, "You can't get that many in the back of a half-ton truck." My less-than-brilliant response (which was all I could think to say) was, 'Well, we don't have a half-ton truck'. Needless to say, I of course should have been locked away for a few years for such reckless 19-year-old behavior with the car and the kids, but he let us go without further concern.

Along with one of the kids in my youth group, I did two motor jobs on the Austin through the summer, but when I carelessly wrecked it on the edge of town there wasn't much value left in it. I had walked away from my car wreck in St. Stephen, New Brunswick, and woke up to the bad press the next morning with the picture and story on the front page of the St. Croix Courier.

With the motor shot and the body wrecked, I suppose I did well to get $17.50 for it at the salvage yard. An hour later, I then put that money towards a bus ticket back to the 'hoped for' safety of Nova Scotia, only to light that fateful fire in the cabin stove a few nights later. Some years later, I looked up a number of the kids from that summer, and they remembered 1965 as, "the best summer we ever had around here".

Did you get assigned any other student pastorates?

Miraculously, yes! When the summer of 1966 was approaching, Rev. Dr. Raymond Whitney of the Home Mission Board, recklessly assigned me again, this time to a Nova Scotia Ministry - the Greenfield Pastorate of Queen's County. This time I didn't smash up my car until the end of the Summer. It happened in Wolfville.

I lived in the parsonage, at least at night. Otherwise, I roamed the countryside all hours of the day. I visited people in the various communities, practicing the convenient, bad habit of showing up at breakfast, dinner or suppertime. However, Mom and Dad modeled those rude manners to me by frequently having the local ministers and visiting ministers in for meals. That Greenfield pastorate was a wonderful experience!

I expect you also did some work?

Yes, I was involved in helping to get the Long Lake Baptist Youth Camp up and running for the summer and then enjoyed helping out with Camp Leadership and meeting some very special people. The official ministry included being Chaplain at the local 'County Home' and looking after the churches in Chelsea, Buckfield, Greenfield and Middlefield.

Were you a good student at Acadia?

Nobody ever accused me of being a Rhodes Scholar. Not only did I find I had to work fairly hard to even pass my courses, but I also didn't actually have much time to study. During my Master of Divinity years (actually called Bachelor of Divinity then, even for the married guys), I actually was a 'roads scholar' you might say; for a year and a half I drove to Truro each weekend to look after the Truro Heights Church. Then when Greenfield, Queens County, asked me to come back again (a couple of years after my student summer placement) I then spent two years traveling that 300 km. round trip each weekend to look after the 4 churches there, plus the County home in Middlefield. Willie Nelson seemed to describe it pretty good when he eventually got his song out, "On the Road Again".

Gary, you mentioned to me several times about your feelings of inadequacy. Did you feel inferior when you were at Acadia University?

It seems I have always felt like others could do everything or anything better than I could. It was almost miraculous to me that I even graduated from high school, let alone getting to Acadia (as it was, I just barely scraped in - and out). On a French test, Albert Einstein only got 3 out of 6 questions right and I like to equate that with me getting a 50 on my grade twelve French exam. I had no background, skills or experience at sports or debating but the basic academics were challenging enough. In my BA days, there were art courses, which were considered so easy that you got automatic credit just by registering for them – I flunked one of them the first term. Theology Classes were often just 5 or 6 students, and I was proud to always finish in the 'top ten'. These feelings of not measuring up seemed to be a part of my DNA. I guess that if hearing and speech (or any other impediments) leave you feeling inadequate and confused, it can colour your self-perception.

How did you feel when you finally got help for your hearing?

When I was a child and Dr. Fraser in Antigonish tested my hearing, I was told a hearing aid would be of no help. At some point in my college years, I was told again there was no help, and that I would slowly lose more of my hearing until I was 65 - whereupon it would deteriorate more rapidly. When I was about 25 or so, Linda suggested I get tested again, in case technology and diagnosis had progressed in that field. We made arrangements to have me tested at H.W. MacKinnon's on Spring Garden Road in Halifax where they told me a hearing aid would help. We went back and picked up the prescribed one, 2 or 3 weeks later. When I got out of the car back at the Greenfield Parsonage, I was amazed to hear the birds singing and the background roar of the nearby Medway River. It has been a great relief to have had some improvement in my hearing over the decades since. Eventually, hearing aid professionals realized that most of us have two ears, so I helped them double their business (in recent years) by getting two at a time. The second one gives a better sense of the direction of a sound, although I still often need to be looking directly at the person I am talking to, in order to catch their exact words.

How often did you get home to Seal Harbour while you were at Acadia and how did you travel?

When I was at Acadia, I got home at Thanksgiving, Christmas and February break for the first years; less so as I became increasingly involved in weekend church responsibilities in Queens County and in Truro. Before I had a car, I mostly travelled by Acadian Lines to and from Antigonish and every once in a while managed a free ride with family or friend for part of the trip.

What highlights of your Acadia days do you remember in particular?

While at Acadia I held (among other duties) the position of president of the Theology Club. It had been our custom to appoint one of the outstanding students to attend the Annual Ecumenical Theological Students Conference over the Christmas break. It was quite an honor for anyone to be appointed as it reflected on their high standing in the School of Theology. Thankfully, none of the bright ones were available to go, so I went. It was my first time on an airplane, first time out of the Maritimes, and I was off to Montreal! Linda and I had just started hanging out a bit at Acadia, so I took a day off and went by bus to Ottawa to visit her and her parents and sister. We all went to Parliament Hill and gathered around the Centennial flame. I lost my gloves somehow in the process.

While at the Conference, I took Wednesday night off and walked down to the Montreal Forum to see my beloved HABS in live action. It was Bobby Orr's first season and Boston and Montreal tied 2–2. It was a great experience for me to be there and see Boom-Boom Geoffrion in action, along with Jean Belliveau, Dickie Moore and Jacques Plante; come to think of it, this turned out to be the only time I would actually attend an NHL game. Between periods, I bravely sauntered into the tavern (or whatever they called it) there at the Forum and sat back and drank the first beer of my life, trying to see if I was comfortable in that milieu or not. However, my strict up- bringing about such things kicked in and I still probably haven't had more than a dozen in my whole life so far. I get into enough trouble sober and didn't dare take the extra risks.

During the Conference, I was interviewed by CBC radio to represent the Baptist point of view but when the program was aired the following week I didn't tell anyone and took Linda skating, rather than suffering the embarrassment of listening to myself being interviewed. The next day Dr. Cherry told me he'd heard the interview and how impressed he was with it.

Gary, other than the chickens, did you have other pets as you were growing up?

We always had a cat or two as part of the family circle. On a cold winter night, one cat in particular served as a warm fur-lined hot water bottle, content to be under the covers at my feet. One day I got terribly concerned about the cat being missing longer than it should. It didn't come when I called it, so I 'took it to the Lord in prayer.' I went into Mom and Dad's bedroom right off the kitchen, knelt down and told the Lord I was terribly worried about the cat and asked if he would please send it back. I got up from the bedside, walked through the kitchen and opened the outside door and there, of course, was the cat, looking rather frazzled, with my own rabbit snare around its neck. Thankfully, I had (in my inexperience) set the snare so poorly that the cat had been able to pull the snare and stick out of the ground and stumble home. You can see the obvious lesson I learned about prayer. And you also see why one of my favorite songs of the time became "The Cat Came Back". Murray Power of Pereaux Church gets a great kick out of that story. (Murray's wife Marion was the long time organist in in the Church, accompanied by Mildred Rand; the 'kids' of both these musicians continue to be wonderfully active in the life of the church).

I was also good friends with our Rosie the Cow. Rosie was the last cow standing in Seal Harbour, when Dad assassinated her in 1957 and then got a car.

(And when I finished laughing uncontrollably…) Who were your heroes when you were a boy - either on TV, real, or imagined?

Thankfully, we didn't get a television till 1960, so I already had established a way of life independent of it and never have really spent much time watching one since, except for news programs. The real world of ocean, woods, community and church were much more interesting to me than artificial entertainment on a screen. I guess I'm still that way. So, I don't recall heroes as such, other than being fascinated by the life of Jesus. In the woods back of our school house we DID have our cowboy trails, where we played Cowboys and Indians and kept killing each other. So, to a degree (and for a while) Roy Rogers, Gene Autry, and the Lone Ranger, were important in our imaginations.

In my early and mid-teens, our various Guysborough County churches had a number of Acadia students as summer ministers who all impacted my life and my sense of a possible calling to the ministry. These included the brothers Bruce and David Watt, Glen Lidstone, John Beers, Keith Churchill and Gordon Delaney. Each of them left lasting impressions and influences on me in their interactions with the people of the churches and communities, including and perhaps especially, the young people. Likewise, my Sunday School teachers Beryl Langley, Mom, Bridget Manthorne, Phoebe

Latham, Clare Fanning, 'Aunt Joy' Manthorne, and of course, Superintendent Dad. Then when Rev. Robert Currie, a black preacher from the United States, became our minister in Seal Harbour itself, it was he who brought me to the Youth Conventions at Acadia for two summers. He also had me involved as a leader in the local Camp Ministry that he started in our area.

As a youngster, I would fervently pray that my brother Charles and I would both make our decision to become Christians at the same time. However, the time came when I took that step at summer camp in Cape Breton. I kept on praying for him and eventually around the age of thirty-three he was baptised at Bayer's Road Baptist Church and has been a devoted church leader ever since.

I would like to have some details about your camp. What was the best thing about it?

In retrospect, the best thing about it was the active hands-on fun of all the years of being outdoors in the woods building and rebuilding something. I cut down small trees for logs, lugged home driftwood from the Atlantic Shore and got scraps of material from Barney Langley, who had torn down his old barn. I built double bunks in it using barrel staves and fox wire, tar- papered the roof which unfortunately wasn't slanted properly - and as a result of such poor design (there was no design), it leaked badly. I ended up with a very make-shift sink with running water in one of my upgrades. The walls were lined with cardboard, so when the decrepit stovepipe and chimney system failed at midnight, Labor Day, 1965, it all burned down in a hurry.

Sharing His Great Love

When did you start building the camp?

I started it when I was 11 years old. The other boys around Seal Harbour would come to hang around and sometimes work on it.

How far was the camp from your house?

Our home was only a couple hundred feet from this huge woods that went for miles, and the camp wasn't very far back in the woods. The hunters would be coming out of the woods at dusk and see my kerosene lamp aglow in the window, so I always liked Max Wiseman's song, "When it's Lamp Lighting Time in the Valley".

What were some other childhood pastimes?

Well, I spent a chunk of my childhood building and rebuilding the camp, rabbit hunting and lobster fishing with my grandfather, hanging out at the fish plant where Dad worked, hanging out with the other kids in the various fish sheds and playing in the sand of the cove.

As a young boy, what did you aspire to be when you grew up?

At one level, I simply expected to live forever in Seal Harbour and either be a fisherman or work in Dad's fish plant. However, Mom and Dad could see ahead and knew that things would be changing in my lifetime and they encouraged me (pushed me) to do the best I could at school. At another level, I found myself at one point (around 8 or 9 years old), writing a sermon on John 3:16. So something was 'clicking' in that realm early on. However, it didn't make sense that a fellow with hearing and speech distortions would think about public speaking. So years later, when I won the Harvey Crowell Public Speaking Contest at Acadia, it was an especially satisfying achievement.

Did you see it as a help or a hindrance to you that your mom was your teacher?
Most of my teachers at the local school 'til Grade 8 were relatives, so it was mostly ok to have Mom as a teacher although I didn't get away with as much under her reign. In Primary, I see that the 20- year-old teacher marked my report card as fine for the 'courses' but it shows that my conduct deteriorated as the year went on.

What would you say was your biggest challenge during your school years?
I took a lot of teasing for my jumbled speech; maybe today it would be called bullying. As a result, I spent much of my life struggling with what we now call self-esteem issues. Perhaps it gave me some appreciation for problems that other people deal with in life. Thankfully, Mom wasn't content to just leave me in that semi-dysfunctional state. Thanks to her commitment to doing what she could to help me, my hearing problem was diagnosed which in turn explained the speech problems. I somehow ended up taking therapy 180 miles away in Halifax with Marie Rudd, and of course back home I had these exercises to work on. I still have the notebook.

That must have been a bit of a strain on family finances.
We didn't have a car or spare cash and there was no MSI in the 1950's, but somehow Mom and Dad got me to Halifax and as a result my speech eventually

improved. However, I never did get help with the hearing problem until I had finished School and University. Maybe if I had heard what was going on in my classes I could have raised my average from a C to a C plus. When I started at Acadia, Dr. Cherry got me into more speech therapy which helped some more.

Did you miss a lot of school to go to Halifax for speech therapy?

I don't think I missed a lot of school to go to Halifax; just a few days at a time. Mom would see that I practiced my exercises to re-learn how to make the sounds correctly.

Were you excited and happy to go to school or did you find it stressful?

As best I can remember, I was always ready, able and willing to go to school. Whatever stress there may have been around it, it seemed important to do the best I could with it.

Gary, you mentioned that Parker Langley came to your rescue when the other kids were teasing you. What sort of things had they said to you, to make Parker want to 'stand up for you?

I really don't know what was said. Perhaps I literally didn't quite hear it, but both he and I knew that it didn't feel good at the time. Not that it was constant - I was good friends most of the time with any of the kids who were within a year or two of my age. I was just confused because I couldn't hear well and I was not sure what the teasing was all about. I was trying to do the best I could and wanted to get along. I suppose that has continued to be my instinctive philosophy of life - to do the best I can, whether it is as good as someone else or not, and to just get along with people.

What about girls as you got older? Did they want you to be their boyfriend?

The girls always wanted me to be their boyfriend, but they made very sure that they never let me or anyone else ever know about it, shall we say.

Well (laughing) that is a great attitude to have about it. Did you go to your School Prom?

The short answer is - no. I was baptized at the age of 13 in the cove next to the fish plant where Dad worked - (It was also next to the cemetery where my grandparents and parents are now buried). I was very serious about the Christian commitment that I gave testimony to, in my baptism. I was always in Church at any opportunity and sometimes I was the only kid there. So, when the minister of the day (like most Baptist ministers of those days) promoted the evils of dancing', I felt I had to buy into it. When I was in Grade 12, he put on an alternative event at prom time (I hardly knew what prom meant) and my hyper-active guilt complex compelled me to do 'the Christian thing'. So, I went to the minister's event. I was the only one who did. Nobody ever told me what went on at the prom. By not going, instead of feeling distorted pride that I was 'Standing up for Jesus', I simply felt more than ever like the oddball I seemed to be in too many ways. It was NOT a good feeling.

What was Christmas like at home Gary?

Thankfully, Christmas was always the exciting, awesome time that it should be for a child. It was a wonderful combination of the joy of Jesus' birth and the mystique of Santa Claus. Mom and our other teachers produced wonderful Christmas Concerts. I still remember my first public speech at the welcome recitation in my first year or so of school; 'Welcome to one, welcome to all, welcome to everyone great and small.'

Do you have memories of your favourite gifts?

Charles and I had our Aunt Phyllis in Toronto come home for Christmas in 1953, and we were in awe of the blue, Rudolph the Red-Nosed Reindeer record player and records that she gave us – they still have a place of honor in my basement den. That was the same Christmas that Grandfather made me my red wheelbarrow which I have displayed at church services over the years.

What was the worst Christmas you ever had?

There was never a bad Christmas, except when Charles and I were in our forties. Mom and Dad had died a few weeks apart in October - November, and I certainly recall that for my household, it was a more somber celebration for sure. How blessed my brother and I were to have had them for all those years.

You almost didn't pass your Ordination exam. What was it that you and Glen Lidstone didn't tell them

that they wanted to hear, or what did you tell them that they didn't want to hear?

Those that voted against us would have wanted us to put things in a more fundamentalist light. Ironically, 4 years later another fellow who was going before them, asked to see my statement so as to get an idea of what to write and say. He basically presented my statement and got along fine. By that point, Ordination procedures weren't the issue of the day.

Who was on the Ordination Board at the time?

Rev. George McNeil was Convention President, Keith Hobson was General Secretary (what we now call Executive Minister); both were on the Board by virtue of their office, as was Dr. Cherry as Dean of Theology (as his job description was then). I can't recall anyone else in particular. Ordination was the current issue of Convention meetings in the late 1960's into 1970 (my year), so we had the feeling the Council was 'gunning' for us. The other fellows (all guys that year) said, "You just tell them what they want to hear and it won't be a problem." Glen and I, being recklessly naïve and idealistic, declared, "No, we're going in to be accepted or rejected for who we really are. We won't dress up our responses."

Author's note:

It is interesting to me how my path intertwined with Gary's without us even knowing it. It makes me think about how really we need to respect other humans and be conscious of the fact that we are all connected, and how our actions, words and thoughts can affect people we have yet to meet.

In the late 1970's, I was the Minister of Youth and Music (along with my late husband, Ken Miller) at Central Baptist Church in Saint John, NewBrunswick. I became good friends with a lovely lady in that church by the name of Rhoda Lidstone. Yes, this was Glen Lidstone's mother. She often asked me to pray for Glen because he was distressed that he could not get a pastorate assignment in the Baptist church. He ended up in my home church which was the United Church in Sheet Harbour. I had met Glen a couple of times and he seemed to be a very pensive, introverted type of guy and the direct opposite in personality to our Gary Manthorne. In retrospect, it could have been that he was depressed, but in any case, sadly, he took his own life, in the United Church Manse. Unknown to us, this connected Rhoda, Gary, me, the Central Baptist Church in Saint John and the little United Church in Sheet Harbour (where I grew up and spent my teenage years teaching Sunday School).

CHAPTER FIFTEEN

Gary, on Family Life and Roots

"We were so delighted to welcome Andrew Paul Manthorne to our Melanson family on July 6th, 1979, born in Wolfville Hospital as was his brother Allan. Just as my father before me, who had two sons about four years apart, each of Dad's two sons now had two sons about four years apart! Andrew immediately showed his lineage on my mother's side with his red hair. Many of Mom's nieces and nephews were red-heads and my beard was red for many years. Andrew followed in my footsteps - by bearing the scars of being the younger brother.

Allan was racing him down two flights of inside stairs when Andrew lost his footing and broke his arm in the fall, requiring surgery later. He broke an arm a couple more times by the time he was six followed by a broken leg at Day Camp at Acadia. Allan, as I wrote earlier, escaped over fences whenever he felt like it - an example set by our dogs. One day, Hugh Fairn showed up at the Gaspereau parsonage door with Allan, who was not even two years old, and said he had found him walking down the road.

The Life and Ministry of Pastor Gary Manthorne

A Devoted Dad

Andrew and Allan

Then when I was building the house a year later, Allan scared the daylights out of his mother. As she was coming along the road in front of the house she saw him standing on the upstairs balcony, before I had gotten to the point of building the rail. I had discovered him at about the same moment and forced myself to remain calm as I beckoned gently to him to come back inside where I was working.

I was still smoking my college pipe once in a while at this early point. One day as I was lighting up, Allan said (in great wisdom for a 4 year old), 'Dad, you say you don't want me to smoke when I get older. Don't you think maybe you're setting a bad example for me?' That was the last puff I had. I wondered at times if someone had rehearsed those lines with him.

The boys had their share of responsibilities. They increasingly took on household chores; not necessarily 'volunteering'. They vacuumed, dusted, made their beds and took shifts on the mowing. One Sunday in Lockhartville Church, when the kids had gone out for Junior Church, I started my sermon by mentioning the various duties the boys carried out. I told the congregation that I sometimes wondered if we were being too hard on them. Andrew poked his head out from behind a door and declared 'You're darn right they're too hard on us.' I was gratified to know that he was listening to my sermon so intently.

In regards to mowing, we had this vacant lot between us and our wonderful neighbours Wayne, Theresa, and Karen Corkum. As the former pasture started growing up with alders after 2 or 3 years, I started clearing and mowing it. Ruby and Basil

Smith, who had owned the whole hillside before selling off most of the other lots, would tell me how nice it looked and how glad they were that I was taking care of it. After a couple years they said, 'You obviously like that piece of land and you have made it look so good. You'd appreciate it more than anyone else. If you'd like to have it, we'll give it you for this very modest amount.' Little had I known when I cleared their land so I'd have a place to play with the boys at soccer and such things, that we'd be rewarded in such an unexpected way. Someone else might have charged me with trespassing on their land.

I was never a cook or baker (although there are Cooks and Bakers in Isaac's Harbour), but I did do some basic meals when the kids were small. I always had breakfast ready for the family. For Sunday suppers I would do up Kraft Pizzas - or Kraft Dinners, depending on the orders. Otherwise, I handled the dish-washing.

Being a father helped me to understand some of the basic philosophical questions my own father had asked me to reflect on - 'Did I think money grew on trees? Did I want to spend the rest of my life in Dorchester Penitentiary? Was I born in a saw mill?'

With the boys taking up skiing on school outings, Linda and I started going along as helpers and soon all four of us were enjoying our investment in a family pass for several years. Learning to ski was, for me, very therapeutic. When you have to concentrate for seven minutes on how you're going to get to the bottom of the hill alive, it wonderfully concentrates the mind and flushes out any lesser concerns of everyday life that might have been pressing in. It seems to me someone famously said that a 'hanging' concentrates one's attention, too. We mainly skied at Martock near Windsor but on a couple of March school breaks we ventured to Wentworth. Andrew spent three years working and skiing at Whistler in British Columbia, quite a contrast to Martock and Wentworth.

In addition to our 3 acre, wooded property in Melanson, we enjoyed our summer vacations in Seal Harbour, at the Greenfield cottage on beautiful Ponhook Lake and later at the Avonport cottage as I renovated it. We had some wonderful trips; several times to Vancouver to visit the family and Expo 86, a cross-country round trip by railroad, and a trip to Toronto in 1988. While in Toronto we visited Niagara Falls where I lost my cap over a railing. After that, any time friends told me they were going there I asked them to watch for it. So far, no-one has come back with my cap or the gloves that I lost at the Centenial Flame at Parliament hill on a previous trip to Ottawa.

On another trip to Ottawa we stopped at the site of the Governor General's residence. For a moment, I was quite impressed with the humility of the dwelling, which seemed about the size of the family home in Seal Harbour. Then one member of the party realised that I was looking at the guard house by the front gates. Way at the back of the manicured grounds, was Rideau Hall, the real Government House.

Allan had the honour of carrying the Olympic Torch in 1988. We had several summer trips to Prince Edward Island, and especially enjoyed

Cavendish Beach. For many summers in a row, while the boys were still home, their grandparents from Vancouver visited us for a couple weeks. That was always a highlight for all of us. My Mom and Dad, living relatively near-by in Seal Harbour, were able to make the four hour drive several times a year. On their way to or from the Valley, they always visited my brother Charles and his wife Gloria in Lakeside, and their other Halifax relatives. For some years, we got family passes for the basketball games at Acadia, which meant that some years we also went to the Metro Centre for the Atlantic Playoffs (and even the National) Playoffs. Other than that, my acquaintance with the Metro Centre was when Alex and I went to hear such Country Music stars as Johnny Cash, Merle Haggard, George Jones and Charlie Pride.

Osborne, one of Dad's brothers, lived most of his life right in Seal Harbour 'trying his hand' at fishing with his father and later mink-ranching. Their other brother, Herman, had left home for Halifax, about the same time as their sister Phyllis did. Before that, as a young man Herman had contracted tuberculosis and spent some time at the Kentville Sanatorium . In 1967, he married a widow named Marjorie, who had 4 children. We were all so pleased for him as they all immediately became a delightfully bonded new unit with one another. After retirement, Uncle Herm and Aunt Marjorie moved to the Valley where three of her daughters were living, and became established citizens of New Minas and of the Valley churches. Uncle Herm, in contrast to Dad and their brother Os, was quite a story-teller - entertaining his new family and us with his anecdotes of life in Seal Harbour as it had been when he was a kid."

CHAPTER SIXTEEN

Conclusions

Recently I received this lovely poem which I believe brilliantly sums up Gary's story.

Reverend Gary

A humble start
in the fog,
scrubby spruce,
rocky coast,
golden bog,
salt in the air,
fish in the sea,
seagulls squawking
and circling above.
In the hearts of the people,
so much love.

Fishing village on Eastern Shore,
who could want for more?
Seal Harbour a place of
freedom and grace.
Rowing in skiffs
in breezes fair,
Goose Island an anchor

The Life and Ministry of Pastor Gary Manthorne

just over there
across The Sound.

Boy became man.
One fine day as
he sat at the table,
he said to his mother
I think I am able
to take up the call
and be an example
of that Jesus fellow
born in a stable.

And so the church
became his home,
inviting him to roam in
the Appled Valley.
He marries and buries
and never wearies of
those sick and tired.
He comes to visit
and often tarries
over coffee or tea.
Loves lemon loaf, too!

A sense of humour
to be admired,
never gets tired of
telling the tale of
setting his camp on fire!
The flames grew higher.
Men came from afar
in search of the source

Sharing His Great Love

of such thick smoke.
It was no joke,
but sparks of laughter
still linger in the air.
Some stories never
grow old.

Enjoys tapping his foot
to a bluegrass tune,
tells kids and grandkids
to come visit again real soon.

A glitch with his hearing,
but he has mastered the art
of listening with his heart.
Like all of us he grapples
with life and the question:

why?

He shines a light along the way,
inviting night to turn to day.
What can any of us say
about this man who doesn't
always have a plan, but
whose off-the-cuff remarks
always rise to the occasion?

We say keep up the great service
(pun sincerely intended),
not just behind the pulpit,
but in everything you do.
We so appreciate you.

The Life and Ministry of Pastor Gary Manthorne

A great guy who
makes us merry –
that's our Reverend Gary.
Jesus would approve.

– Bethany B. Keddy

April 2013

Gary Today
Mathew 6:25

"Therefore I tell you, do not worry about your life, what you will eat or drink, or about your body, what you will wear. Isn't there more to life than food and more to the body than clothing?"

Apple Blossom Time in the Annapolis Valley

"It is so wonderful to be living and ministering in the Valley all these years; fifty years after starting at Acadia, 5 minutes from our home here in Melanson. I feel very blessed to have grown up in Seal Harbour with the woods and ocean and still going back and forth from the Valley several times a year. Of course it wasn't all sunshine. Like the fog along the Eastern Shore and the dangers of the sea, I've had some hard sailing on the ocean of life. I would never have imagined for example, that I would ever be divorced, let alone twice. Both of those developments (before, during and after) were times of great inner struggle and darkness for me.

In the spirit of the Psalmist, I wrote volumes of prayers and journals about it all, challenging myself to put one foot ahead of the other, to keep moving and to not succumb to it all. I read and re-read a lot of helpful books that gave me insight into myself. I have never been one who could read something and remember it. I'd have to read it over and over many times. That was true in school, in university, in seminary and in plain-old everyday life. I did a lot of prayerful, meditative thinking from these books and from the Bible. I would jot down in my journals daily the most helpful thoughts, quotes or verses. Then for some time afterwards, I'd keep going back over and over my notes, re-enforcing the lessons I was learning and finding increasing inner peace and contentment. During the process, I kept pushing myself as much as I could to do the basic work of the ministry. In the midst of it all, I was nurtured by a sense of the spiritual reality of the Christian faith, underlined by the wonderful support of my many communities and some very special dear friends.

Through decades in the ministry, a lot of precious people have shared some of their struggles with me. I value that trust and consider it a privilege. As I think of what other people have gone through, I would not have wanted to handle the things they had to deal with, just as they might have preferred their own problems to mine. I am saying something profound there, but of course, I am not quite sure what it is.

The day that brought the tears however, was when Haley Dawg (Dawg being the dog's sir name) died of old age. She and I had been great companions through the years. We'd go on long walks, often late at night. I'd tell her my troubles and I'd tell her my blessings. I'd sing hymns and country music songs to her. She was amazingly non-judgmental and supportive of all my thoughts and feelings, never howled at my singing, didn't recommend I take medication or get into alcohol and all she ever seemed to want for counseling fees were biscuits and massages.

I slowly but surely started coming into a more peaceful focus and could increasingly reassure myself that the depressing moments or hours would pass. I loved the verse of St. Paul who testified that he could do all things through Christ who strengthened him. I realised I didn't even have to do ALL things and that with Christ within me, I could do what I needed to do and could live my life with inner peace and joy. Now I seldom have a low moment, let alone low days or weeks or months. I keep counting my multitude of blessings, following the basic points of the Christian faith, letting go of the regrets of the past, and 'taking no thought' for and having no worry about tomorrow.

When I first came to the Gaspereau Valley churches - Gasperau, Wallbrook and White Rock, in the fall of 1972, Willie and Marguerite Biggs were always in Church at Wallbrook, and sometimes daughters Donna, Shirley and Shirley's husband Lowell would also be there when home on weekends. In 1983, Donna called me from Toronto to see if I might conduct her wedding at the Acadia Chapel in December. I was happy to do so. She and George lived in Toronto at that time and indeed continued to do so 'till George's death in 2000. In 2005, Donna (from Toronto) and Shirley and Lowell (from Fort McMurray) moved back to Nova Scotia from their established lives and families to be available to help out their parents who were by that time getting up in years and no longer for example, driving to their errands.

By quite the interesting coincidence, Willie and Marguerite were by that time living across the road from my present residence. By now, I had been separated and divorced the second time. Seeing Donna driving in and out of her parents' driveway on their frequent errands together, it occurred to me to check with her as to whether she'd like to go for an ice cream, based on the ancient courting ritual of Seal Harbour. We had each decided by then that there'd be no more marriages at our advanced stages. But, we had made allowance for maybe keeping company with someone if they met certain requirements. One of mine was that the woman live within a 15 minute drive. Turned out, Donna's home in Black River was a 17 minute drive. Always being bit flexible on such principles, I stretched my regulations and it ended up that we 'saw each other' for two years before suddenly declaring, 'let's get married' which occurred in my back yard here in Melanson on June 30th, 2012, with only Lowell, Shirley and Mr. and Mrs Biggs in attendance. Rev. Pauline Coffin officiated. We announced it to Pereaux and Forest Hill churches the next day and then came home and told the rest on Facebook. We had decided that our home would be the house I had been in for the previous 3 plus years across from her folks. Her own house in Black River had already been up for sale before we started going out.

Linda and Rachel had gotten married the previous September and they live in the family home I built in 1978, just down the hill a kilometer from Donna and me. We all get along fine and it's a great set-up when the family comes in from Halifax or Yarmouth, for us all to go freely back and forth between the two homes. Sometimes Donna and I look after Linda and Rachael's tiny Misty Dawg. It is really cute when the tiny Misty and Andrew and Erin's huge Golden Lab, Molly, both come and stay with us for several days when their respective owners are away.

Allan and Kayleigh in Yarmouth have a delightful Uzi Dawg, that we enjoy seeing when we go there. But of course best of all is when Allan's kids, Taylor and Tyson, come and visit with us and with Linda and Rachael down the hill. In the summers of 2011 and 2012, Donna and I shared the delights of Seal Harbour with them. They got a great kick out of finding that there was a Manthorne Settlement so far from their home in Yarmouth. They were also excited to learn that they were related to Arch and his extended family and to the dozens of Manthornes at rest in the cemetery. They immediately started cleaning up some of the gravestones, so as to make their family name clear for all to see.

Gary, Donna, Tyson and Taylor

It is a wonderful blessing to have Donna as my best friend and wife. Perhaps the most public demonstration of her interest and support for me was the surprise party she co-ordinated for me at Forest Hill Church on October 16th, 2011, the 41st anniversary of my Ordination. I was planning to make reference to my Ordination at the 2:30PM service but was not expecting anyone extra to be on hand. So when we came within site of the church with Dr. Cherry aboard, I was shocked to see dozens of cars in the parking lot and I suddenly realised what was going on (or thought I did). I blurted out, 'Donna, you are so evil', an accusation I may not have ever said to anyone who DID deserve it. Dr. Cherry chuckled at my distorted theology knowing as he did what was going on. We went inside and I did my service, as planned, enjoying seeing so many friends and family from all directions. They came from as far away as Yarmouth, Guysborough County, and Greenfield in Queens County. In 1970, Greenfield had been the site of the actual Ordination Service.

After I gave the Benediction, organist Heather leaned over to me and said to my hearing aids, 'Actually, I think it's just getting started.' Indeed, for another 3 ½ hours we had special music, presentations, comments, tributes and anecdotes from the various churches represented from over the years. The heart-warming display amazed me and almost made me wonder at times who this person was that they were talking about.

And now, Heather is causing me to feel the same way by taking on this project. There are lots of worthy people around deserving of the attention. I thank God for His blessings, I thank Heather for the honour she has bestowed upon me and I thank all of you who make my life so precious and meaningful. I appreciate your loyalty, friendship and unconditional love.

As much as I wish Mom and Dad had lived an extra quarter century to read this book, it is maybe just as well this way; Charles and I were brought up in such a way that you never bragged about anything to do with yourself or the family and if anything, you looked down on those you felt thought a little too much of themselves and considered them haughty.

When I would come home in the summer and preach at a church service, Mom would tell me afterwards about positive things people said about me or my sermon. Dad would follow-up with, 'What else would you expect them to say to you?' When Dad ran for Guysborough Municipal Council and won (in 1958 or so) and Charles was driving us back home from the hall, blowing the car horn in celebration, Dad scolded, 'Cut that out, I'm in enough trouble already.'

In 1973, thinking I finally had an opportunity to make him proud of me and he'd have to say so, I informed him that I was following in his footsteps and was running for Kings County Council. His response was, 'Why are you doing something so foolish?' Thankfully, I lost the election by forty votes. In hindsight, I would have made a very poor councillor as I simply have no instinct or ability to sit around in a circle helping hammer out policies and decisions. My only joy as a councillor would have been in 'hob-knobbing' with the public. The hard work behind the scenes was better left to the previous councilor, Chet Davidson, to Clyde Murray (who defeated me in the election) or to such competent future politicians such as MLA and Cabinet Minister Mark Parent.

On a recent visit to my dad's sister Phyllis in Toronto, I told her that Heather was writing a book about me. Instead of replying, 'I am not surprised' or 'That's quite an honour', her reaction was, 'How come?' - She was being true to the family heritage of being proud of humility."

Gary and Aunt Phyllis

AUTHOR'S CONCLUSION

I understand Gary's upbringing, as in this regard it was similar to mine. I set aside THAT thinking as I grew older. I now believe that God's gift to us is our talent and abilities, and our gift to God is to use that talent and those abilities to the utmost and give him the glory. I assured Gary that the purpose for this book is to show God's favour on his life. However, Gary had choices to make and every choice that was in God's will for his life was divinely directed. It is wonderful to know how God uses us when we let him lead.

I consider it an honour and a privilege to have been able to chronicle, organise and present this material on the life of Gary Manthorne. I hope you will recognise this as a story of triumph over adversity and that it will help you, and generations to come, to understand that of ourselves we can do nothing, but in partnership with a God who sees the whole picture, we can do anything.

Perhaps you recognise the pain, the embarrassment and the frustration of the little boy known as Gary Manthorne. Children learn to speak from hearing others, but Gary could not hear well. Therefore, when he spoke, others struggled to understand. Some people, when they don't understand others and don't know how to respond, react by laughing to lessen the tension or by simply ignoring and isolating the person.

As a boy, Gary had already learned that God answers prayer. He asked God in a simple request to bring his cat back, and he did. He prayed that both he and his brother Charlie would accept Christ at the same time. Instead of thinking that God didn't answer that prayer, he persisted in praying for his brother Charles, and Gary learned that sometimes prayers are answered in God's timing. He also believed God to provide a hospital room for Keith Luddington, when Keith was in need.

God was already tugging at Gary's heart to enter the ministry even while he was still a young boy, when he wrote a sermon on John 3:16. Then, the negative doubts of his perceived short-comings set in. How could anyone with the learning disabilities of poor hearing and speech ever be a preacher? However, God had been preparing Gary all of his life and placing the right people along side of him, who would help him. I don't believe that God would ever give us the desire for something without giving us the ability to complete it. That would be cruel and that is not the kind of God we have.

I believe that generations of blessings have been placed upon Gary and because of the 'Godly walk' of his parents and grandparents he was able to walk with God's favour upon him. Parents, if you wish your children to grow up as the Bible says, 'in the way they should go', they ought to be able to see you walking that path some of the time.

When Gary left Seal Harbour for the town of Wolfville and Acadia University, he must have felt relieved to have a 'clean slate' to write on. However, that feeling was short-lived when at the dining hall, while Gary was laughing and speaking in his usual loud voice, he heard someone say in a loud voice, "Gary Manthorne is that you? I would know that voice anywhere." The all-too familiar feeling of inadequacy and fear swept over Gary when he realised his past was still close beside him.

I believe your past will never leave you. I have learned that you either have to embrace it, and be anchored there, or take the good things (like the lessons learned) and move on, leaving the rest behind. That is what Gary Manthorne did, with God's help. The good things are 'light baggage' and easy to carry.

Gary is deeply rooted in his ancestry and not only was he the first pastor to be licenced to preach in the Seal Harbour Church, recently, he was the only pastor (of the many invited) to return to Seal Harbour for a reunion. He visits there regularly. His family is very important to him and he takes great joy in his children and grandchildren. I am sure they walk under the blessings that Gary will pass down to them and that will make their journey just a bit little easier.

Many of us, if in the same situation, would have quit way before now. We would have made excuses of our challenges and remained in the seclusion of our homes as fisherman in the village of Seal Harbour. But God had plans to make Gary a 'fisher of men' and Gary kept on following. This, I believe, was Gary's secret. He didn't see the big picture. He knew he had limitations put upon him physically and emotionally, through no fault of his own, and he chose to just keep on following God's prompting. Can you imagine what a different scene it would be in the Valley if it were not for a ministry such as Gary's? Who would people call for the funeral of an un-churched loved one?

As I have said previously, I have attended many of the funerals that Gary has conducted over the years. Gary always presides with love, and makes the event about the person. He does not try to 'preach' them into heaven, nor does he condemn them. He probably thinks it is not his job, and I agree.

Many of us have given in to limitations, either real or imagined, but it is never too late to 'dust off' our dreams and set about to make something happen. Gary just kept plodding ahead which seems to be all God requires of us for him to create the environment for the fulfillment of our dreams. Where have you buried your dreams? Gary didn't bury his, he planted them, watered them and God gave the harvest. He will do the same for you.

I mentioned to Gary a poem, by Rudyard Kipling, that I think exemplifies Gary's life from the worldly prospective. Gary told me that years ago he had a little red autograph book in which his father had written the beginning lines of that exact same poem. I hope you will look up the poem and read it in its entirety. It is called simply "If". It starts, "If you can keep your head when all about are losing theirs and blaming it on you"…and it ends with… "You will be a man my son."

Congratulations Gary and Thanks!

Sharing His Great Love

Subject Gary and Author Heather at the 30th
Seal Harbour Reunion, Tea Party by the Shore

Ladies at the Tea Party by the Shore

RESOURCES:

All scripture verses are taken from the New English Translation Bible.

Poem – One, Two, Three, Four, Five - Roud Folk Song Index #13530 – c.1765 Lines from "If" by Rudyard Kipling

Dr. Gardner's Bio:

Dr. Harry G. Gardner, a native of the south shore of Nova Scotia, graduated from Dalhousie University (BA 1974), Acadia Divinity College (MDiv 1977) and from Fuller Theological Seminary, Pasadena, California (DMin.1993). He has served as the minister of the Burlington- Victoria Harbour and Wilmot and Liverpool-Brooklyn United Baptist Churches.

In 1986 he began work with the Home Mission Board of the Convention of Atlantic Baptist Churches and in 1989, became the Director of Home Missions and Church Planting. For the past 11 years, he has served as the Convention's Executive Minister. In this role, he was a member of the Boards of Acadia Divinity College and Atlantic Baptist University. He has had a keen interest in addressing issues of racism, promoting integral mission, as well as international relief and development. Recently, he was the president of the

North American Baptist Fellowship and a member of the executive of the Baptist World Alliance. In January 2008 he began as president of Acadia Divinity College and the Dean of Theology for Acadia University.

He and his wife Gail, reside in Kentville. Their family includes two married children and three grandchildren. Personal interests include fun times with the grandchildren, travel and music.

OBITUARY OF DR. MILLARD CHERRY:

The Reverend Doctor Millard Ross Cherry, affectionately known to all as "Cherry", died on Friday, October 5th, 2012 in the Valley Regional Hospital, Kentville. Cherry was born in Franklin, Simpson County, Kentucky on December 2nd, 1921. He was baptised as a teenager and licensed to preach at 19. He served as Pastor from age 20, in the State of Arkansas and later in Taylorsville, Kentucky. Cherry held a B.A. from Ouachita Baptist University (1944), a B.D. (1948) and a Doctor of Theology (1957) degree from Southern Baptist Seminary in Louisville, Kentucky. In 1957 Cherry made a significant decision to come to Canada where he became Professor of Systematic Theology in the school of theology at Acadia University. He deeply cherished his Canadian citizenship, which was granted in 1970. Cherry's contribution to Nova Scotia, and beyond, had been truly remarkable. At Acadia, he served on numerous boards and committees over a twenty- five year period. Especially notable, was his service as Dean of Theology (1963-71) the first principal of Acadia Divinity College (1968-71) and the associate dean of Acadia Divinity College (1971-80).

In recognition of his outstanding contribution to Canadian Theological Education, he received three honorary degrees from Pine Hill Divinity Hall (1970), McMaster Divinity College (1982) and Acadia University (1988). Cherry made a vital contribution to denominational and ecumenical life, serving the United Baptist Convention of the Atlantic Provinces on the Standards for Ordination and Candidates Committee, the Credentials Committee, the Ordination Council and the Recruiting Committee. In addition, he was a popular guest lecturer and preacher in seminaries and churches of several denominations across Canada. Following retirement from Acadia, Cherry was an interim pastor at the Wolfville Baptist Church and St. Andrews United Church, Wolfville, (1988). He then pastored Pereaux Baptist Church (1988-94). Cherry was predeceased by his father Daniel Borthic Cherry, his mother Nema Brown Hatter Cherry and his brother, Billy Jeff (Ruth) Cherry. He is survived by his nephew Daniel Potts (Danita) Cherry and their children Laurn, Jeffrey and Alexander, all of Kentucky. Though a bachelor, Cherry was a devoted and fatherly mentor to generations of students and their families. He eagerly and generously offered unconditional love, in his role as counselor and friend, and his ecumenical spirit was particularly cherished by all who knew and loved him. To celebrate his 80th birthday in 2001, over 400 friends assembled, at Atlantic Theatre Festival in Wolfville, to honour Cherry for his contribution to the Acadia University family, the people of Annapolis Valley and far beyond. At this time, Cherry was honoured with a life membership in the Wolfville Rotary Club and a Paul Harris Fellowship in tribute to "his special qualities as a person of unusual warmth, kindness, community spirit and service." More recently, Cherry was inducted into Acadia University Sports Hall of Fame in recognition of his many years as an ardent supporter and encourager of all Axe teams. His funeral was conducted by Rev. Gary Manthorne and Rev. Dr. Mark Parent at the Pereaux Baptist Church with a reception in the hall named after him – Cherry Hall.

Heather Ann Card was born Heather Ann Spears in Sheet Harbour, N.S. Canada in 1947. She has been a writer, speaker and musician for most of her life. Although "Sharing His Great Love" is her first published book, Heather has written many training manuals and is known online as an expert writer of short articles at ezine.com. She has been involved in Christian Ministry since her teenage years of playing the organ and teaching Sunday School. Heather worked in the Rothesay Baptist Church in N.B. as Choir Director and in Central Baptist Church in Saint John N.B. as Music Director and Director of Youth Ministry.

Presently she is a volunteer organist with Forest Hill Baptist Church near Wolfville where she occasionally has the opportunity to fill in for the pastor. Heather is the mother of five adult children, the stepmother to another and the grandmother of 9. She lives with her husband Lloyd on Gaspereau Mountain, near Wolfville, N.S., Canada.

Printed in Canada